Faulkner's Fictive Architecture
The Meaning of Place
in the Yoknapatawpha Novels

Studies in Modern Literature, No. 67

A. Walton Litz, General Series Editor

Professor of English
Princeton University

Joseph Blotner, Consulting Editor

Professor of English
University of Michigan

Other Titles in This Series

Faulkner's Fictive Architecture
The Meaning of Place
in the Yoknapatawpha Novels

by
William T. Ruzicka

Illustrations by
R. B. Ferrier

UMI Research Press

Ann Arbor / London

Produced and distributed by
UMI Research Press
an imprint of
University Microfilms, Inc.
Ann Arbor, Michigan 48106

Library of Congress Cataloging in Publication Data

Ruzicka, William T., 1944-
Faulkner's fictive architecture.

(Studies in modern literature ; no. 67)
Revision of thesis (Ph.D.)—University of Dallas,
1984.
Bibliography: p.
Includes index.
1. Faulkner, William, 1897-1962—Settings.
2. Yoknapatawpha County (Imaginary place)
3. Regionalism in literature.   4. Local color in
literature.   5. Cities and towns in literature.
6. Southern States in literature.   7. Setting
(Literature)
PS3511.A86Z96527   1987   813'.52   87-10799
ISBN 0-8357-1788-7 (alk. paper)

Contents

vi   *Contents*

Figures

All figures have been rendered by R. B. Ferrier, A.I.A.

Introduction: Fictive Architecture

Across Yoknapatawpha's landscape lies a group of built structures and natural places which have remained relatively unnoticed. Reader and critic alike seem to take them as much for granted as the real architecture of everyday life. Yet Yoknapatawpha's barns, cabins and houses, and Jefferson's town square and civic buildings are objects as meaningful as any symbolic or metaphorical phenomenon in the fictive county's inventory. The recent advent of phenomenological study in architectural space and place has begun to allow the application of its methodology and conclusions to the critical study of imaginative space and place. This work attempts to study William Faulkner's fictional Yoknapatawpha County with a view to explicating its fictive architecture. It also seeks to show, with care, how such study should be done.

The whole subject of what demands to be called fictive architecture is part of the larger relationship between the art of the builder and the art of the poet.

Architecture and poetry are two achievements of the same gesture of the human spirit: the effort to embody meaning in a concrete image. One of man's most fundamental needs is to experience his existence, including his environment, as meaningful. This need predicates the concretization of meaning in both poetic and architectonic forms,[1] for it is only in the making of things, or what Heidegger calls the "setting-into-work of truth," that the meaning of things or the truth of Being is "let be."[2] The poet perceives a meaningful insight into the truth and focuses it in the concrete image of the poem. The man who builds perceives a meaningful vision of his environment and focuses it in the built thing. By experiencing places as meaningful, man is said to dwell, and his constructions are called architecture.[3]

By concretizing the meaningful relationships of his existence on the earth into a structure which expresses his world, man makes a gesture in what Christian Norberg-Schulz calls "expressive space." Expressive space comprises any free construction or natural formation of space which signifies, represents or symbolizes some part or act of existence. It is a shaping of space to be an image of the truth.[4] Architectural space is a form of expressive or artistic space and a concretization of existential space, the space of human existence, "man's image of the environment."[5]

The act of concretizing meaning is a poetic act, and the creation of imaginative space in literature is another form of expressive space. It focuses meaning in an *imago mundi*, concretizing meaning in the built forms and imaginative space of the story. As an image of the world, literature has within it, as part of its purpose, all the matter of existence (including architectural matter, built and unbuilt environment) at all the levels perceived in the empirical world: landscape, city, town, house, room, furniture and object. The author as architect of his fictive structures is also the creator of the landscape and topography, even the world and the cosmos within which his characters dwell. Imagined architecture is, for poet, author, character, and even reader, as real as physical architecture. As a concretization of the psychic world of its inhabitants (who are also its participants), imagined architecture includes all the natural and man-made elements and levels of the environment; forest and river as well as mansion and shack.[6] Fictive landscape is an image of the natural world, and as fictive architectural space is the concretization of the fictional characters' existential space, a concretization of the psychic world of its inhabitants, fictive landscape, region and cosmos become analogs for nothing less than ontological space, the space of all Being. Imaginative architecture occurs in poetry, drama and fiction, but it is the novel which presents the most complete and detailed use of imaginative architecture as a symbol system. The critical study of fictive architecture, the imaginative space of fiction, includes exegesis of the house, the landscape and the room as representative objects, as well as consideration of phenomena such as an aura or an environment in terms of their intentional significance.

Critical writing on imaginative architecture seems to be concerned chiefly with the English manor house tradition. Works by Richard Gill and others have studied the English country house and its way of life as rendered in the poetry and fiction of Jonson, James, Galsworthy, Yeats, Woolf, and Waugh.[7]

The presence of these phenomena throughout all of fiction mandates a more thorough critical study of the nature and scope of fictive architecture in its various levels from landscape to domestic object. With these beginnings in the subject of fictive architecture, the close study of the relationships among fictional characters, landscapes, and habitable structures within the work of other individual authors should follow. Novelistic architecture focuses meaning for characters as well as for readers. It has much to say about the way that characters view the world they inhabit, the effect of the fictive environment upon those who live within it, the image and significance of a fictive place, and the meaning of dwelling there.

The importance of fictive architecture derives from the phenomenological nature of imaginative space. Norberg-Schulz's definition of architectural space (as the concretization of man's existential space) may be extended to architectural structures within a novel. The way that such symbolization functions is the same in the genre of the novel as it is in factual architecture. Again, the phenomenological study of architectural space and place provides an analogous explanation of the process. In freely constructing a natural or man-made fictive place, the author either visualizes the intended significance, complements what is already a meaningful place, or symbolizes expressly what significance the place has.

A fictive dwelling can embody the builder's existence, his person, or his family's significance. Almost inevitably it must express something about those who dwell in or near it. Built or unbuilt forms may function as analog (by the actions performed within them), as image (by the visual form they present), as icon (by their resemblance), or as symbol (by partaking of the reality they represent). They can be imagined, planned, dreamed of, built, lived in or died in, added to, burnt, rebuilt, destroyed, cursed or blessed, remembered or forgotten, given, taken away, or lost. And though it is houses which seem to attract most consideration, the surrounding natural world created by the author is a large sphere in which meaning can also be focused into significance at many levels.

The levels of fictive space, like those of the real world, are natural (region and landscape) and man-made (city, town, village, settlement, building, house, room and thing).[8] The fictive natural place is composed of some landscape or portion of a landscape, together with the particular elements which are its content; the ground (its texture, color, and cover), the mountains, trees, rivers and lakes which characterize it, and the daily, seasonal and annual rhythms which create its atmosphere. Fictive landscape is the environmental ground on which characters enact their existence. Its scale might be as large as a region or as small as the dimensions of a formal garden. As a region or a topos, it may generally characterize a community or intimately involve a single protagonist. The paths, enclosures, or open areas on its surface become patterns which may analogize the wanderings of a character or the movement of a soul. We may even speak of topological genres or kinds of landscape—such as a lyric or tragic landscape—where surface patterns depict the formal movements of literature.

Fictive man-made place is formed by the same processes of visualization, complementation and symbolization. The fictive city is large-scale man-made imaginative space, and usually contains several smaller-scale places within it. Seldom is the character or reader familiar with the complete imagined city, but each city is nevertheless a whole, structured, identifiable place. Variations in density and in shape give each its character. Structurally, the centers are the city squares, the paths are the streets, usually in grid patterns, and the areas are urban districts or neighborhoods. Characters show a certain familiarity with a domain known as a neighborhood, distinguished from other areas in the city, and the crossing of certain boundaries may place the protagonist outside his domain and inside an area where he may not belong. Much of the fiction of Dostoevsky takes place at the urban level. Though for Tolstoy life in the country is the good life, Yi-Fu Tuan notes that, "Dostoevsky, by contrast, is wholly immersed in the city. The city may be the inferno but salvation does not lie in the land; it can be found only in the Kingdom of God [with the individual rather than through man's contact with the earth, as in Tolstoy and Faulkner]. Dostoevsky's fiction has few landscapes."[9]

Town, village and settlement are smaller-scale clusters which usually suggest the notion or sense of community. The act of founding a town, as will be seen later, is an epic gesture, and the size and composition of the space formed may have much to say about the nature of the community which formed it.

The house is a concretization of the basic unit of community, the family. "The house gives man his place on the earth,"[10] as well as a local habitation and a name. Where a house has public character as well, it is "an extension of the private world."[11] The mansion of a plantation novel is a particularly intense example. As it is usually placed on a hill overlooking the domain, it reflects the landed man's existential position in the world. It is a visual icon for all his patriarchy, while the classical orders or columns of the house are the conventional sign of his governance of the community.[12] In Faulkner's short story "Barn Burning," for instance, Major Cassius de Spain's white house is linked, in the mind of young Sarty Snopes, with a courthouse by similarity of conventional signs and structure. Both concretize for him the same intention and significance: they are the embodiment of the sense of right order and justice which begins to pull him away from his blood ties.[13] In general, the building of a manse and the establishment of a home within it are the expressions of the existential state of patriarchy. If this condition is expressed on the outside—the public facade of the house—in conventional symbol or otherwise, then the house is an image of the patriarch's place in the community.[14]

The significance of a mansion as a two-story dwelling can be understood from certain integral elements within it. First, despite all the land at his disposal, the builder decides to go *up* with his building. Second, such a house requires a stairway, with all the connotations that ascending stairs imply: ascent in station, public downstairs and private upstairs,[15] together with all the empirical, iconic, and conventional relationships mentioned earlier. Third, the higher up one goes, the more private and philosophical, even sacred, the space becomes. The cherished relics of ancestors and the treasures of the past are kept in the attic, and it is there that Faulkner's Bayard Sartoris, for instance, goes to meet the ghosts of his own past. The interior of the house is more significant of the private world of its inhabitants, and the structure and spatial arrangement of the interior spaces are an image of the way of life pursued within. Interior space may be spoken of in terms of enclosure, centralization, continuity, direction, and symmetry.[16] Within interior space are the objects which articulate the character of the house as an expression of those who dwell within it. Certain items such as the hearth, the table, and the bed are archetypal objects around which the family gathers or to which they turn for the fundamental needs of warmth, food, and rest. Even the everyday tools and objects of common existence become significant in a fictive environment. A gate or a lamp, a compass and watch, carriage and harness, pistol and knife might be included in the catalog of representative objects in the fictive landscape.

The various levels of architectural space exist one within the other, and are interactively related. It is difficult to *be* in one level without being associated with another. The entrance of a house, the threshold, for instance, expresses a relationship between the interior of the house and the world outside.[17]

This structured, analytical organization of the elements and levels of fictive architecture makes it possible to explicate their topological, natural, structural, and artifactual forms, as well as their historical, symbolic, and archetypal associations. A phenomenological approach of this kind is most responsible to the kind of intense significance that the poetic nature of fictive architectural phenomena provides.

William Faulkner's Yoknapatawpha fiction is a rich field for the study of fictive architecture because it depicts a particularly multifarious and intricate, unified and homogeneous community. To approach Faulkner's imaginative world it is necessary to understand how he used imagined places and structures in his fiction. Standard remark on Faulkner's region and landscape usually concerns itself with the inconsistencies of his Yoknapatawpha map or its parallels to Lafayette County.[18] But the important point to remember here is that a created fictional world owes its validity not to some correspondence with a geographical or historical place, but to its own inherent meaning, a particular *genius loci* it possesses irregardless of the fact that a correspondent and similar real world exists. Though explication of fictive architecture in general and Yoknapatawpha in particular have suffered from such comparison, architectural phenomenology now provides an adequate way to make the subject more readily addressable.

The reasons for Faulkner's particular talent in the use of fictive space and place are numerous and related. Several are characteristics of the native Southerner.[19] There is, for one thing, an intense perception and understanding of history not as dates and facts, but in a "personal and dramatic" way, through the stories of family ancestors and their involvement in the political and social nurturing of the country. Together with the natural image- and myth-making tendency of the Southern mind, and an understanding of the nature of symbolism (including architectural representation), this consciousness of the past produced in Southern literature a natural propensity for historical novels.[20]

The fictive architecture of Southern novelists derives its clarity and concreteness from two traditions, one within the other, in which the architecture of the South rests: the English manorial tradition and the Classical Christian tradition of its culture, both inherited from the Old World. The historical development of the Southern architectural tradition from Vitruvius through Alberti, Bramante, Palladio, Sir Christopher Wren, and on to Thomas Jefferson and the Greek Revival style is outside the scope of these pages. But many of the significant aspects can be deduced from looking at the Classical tradition as the *genius loci* of Southern architecture,[21] and at its literary product, the plantation novel. The specific occurrence of Greek Revival architecture in the American South was not, as in the Northern states, a matter of style, but rather the particular response of a culture which understood itself to be a repetition and not an imitation, a recurrence rather than a recreation of ancient Greece, and fortuitously found the architectural style proper to its image. Or, it might rather be said that the style which came to reign, albeit for other reasons, over the entire nation happened to be for the South the embodiment of its own social, political and cultural paradigm. Antebellum Southern architecture in particular showed an exceptional capacity for representational value, and the extent to which such symbolization can be employed in the mode of fiction is seen in the works of William Faulkner. Underlying his art is a sensitive awareness of architecture's ability to signify, a constant and natural part of the artist's understanding of symbolism. Faulkner's imaginative county is the fictive embodiment of the classical vision of his milieu, wrought from a society that already possessed the capacity to embody its ideals in architecture.

1

Background: The Classical
Genius Loci of Southern Architecture

There is in the American South a body of convictions and beliefs which emanate from its close affinity to the Classical world.[1] Part of this body of knowledge—the most important part in dealing with Faulkner's imaginative arena—is that which makes up the *genius loci* of the American South: the convictions and beliefs concerning how natural and man-made places embody meaning. The study of Southern spirit of place applies to all parts of the region, and provides the background for detailing the nature and characteristics of Faulkner's fictive county.

The relationship of Southern natural and man-made places to Greek architectural thinking reveals an affinity of intention in its landscape and built forms. Both the Classical world and the American South possessed a sensitivity to meaningful place, deriving from an older kind of religiousness and its accompanying piety for the natural world. In both the myth and ritual of ancient Greece, natural elements and landforms were invested with the names of the invisible presences felt to inhabit them.[2] In his study of the various kinds of natural places found on the earth, Christian Norberg-Schulz characterizes the Classical landscape, the landscape inhabited with a Classical *genius loci*, as "an intelligible *composition* of distinct elements...a meaningful order of distinct, individual places."[3] By coming to know a natural world of human scale and dimension, Greek man came to know himself and to see the natural world as a complement to his own being. Such an attitude is accompanied by a submission to the mysteries of nature and a fundamental respect for the laws by which it works. There is little or no concern here for "improving" nature: the emphasis is on allowing nature to *be* itself.[4]

The Classical spirit of man-made place in the South, in particular the South of William Faulkner's milieu, reveals itself in the topological and orthogonal organization of its architectural structures. In architectural space, the elements of place, path, and domain form an integrated whole referred to as a *field*. A field composed of square and rectangular structures on a grid

Figure 1-1. Hadrian's Villa with Nonorthogonal Axes
(Based on Sigfried Giedion, Architecture and the Phenomenon of Transition [*Cambridge: Harvard University Press, 1971*]*)*

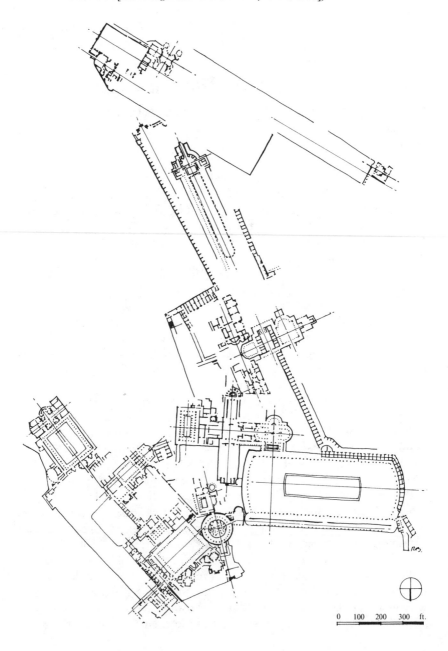

0   100   200   300   ft.

pattern of streets and paths derives from the more formal influence of later Hellenistic Rome. "In Greek architecture, however, [the] interrelation [of axes and paths forming complex fields of places and domains] is less important than the pronounced individuality of each element, whereas in Roman architecture a strong wish for spatial integration is evident."[5]

The South's architectural vision was in general more Greek than Roman, more central than linear, more enclosed than continuous. It may be compared to the Northern states as Greece might be compared to Rome, China to Japan, or England to America: As a culture rather than a civilization. Greek architecture, concerned with mass and volume, built temples to the gods, where the Romans, with surface and linear architecture, built roads and aquaducts, and civic-political architecture as monuments to men. The South had a greater liking for the temple than the viaduct.[6] Its architecture reflected a society more closed than open, more communal and regional than imperial. As a result, architectural structures in the South exhibit a Greek topological arrangement in the smaller hamlets and farms[7] and orthogonal and geometric arrangements in the towns and larger plantations,[8] though individual elements retain emphasis. "In classical Greek architecture," Norberg-Schulz notes, "the organizing relations are tied to the single building, while Hellenistic-Roman architecture knows more extensive compositions like *fora*, baths and palaces."[9] This point is particularly important when considering topologically organized plantation space. In the cultural structure of the South, the space of everyday existence is based on the domain, reflecting the family as the center. The typical nineteenth-century Southern farm is demonstrably topological, with a free but balanced distribution of central house and outbuildings over the site.[10] Though the arrangement of structures usually has a modicum of orthogonal design, the center of the domain is always the planter's house, around which the outbuildings are situated, often at right angles, but seldom symmetrically. Axially symmetrical geometric arrangements developed only with the larger scale cane and cotton plantations of the deep South. That is, the scale of the plantation had as much (if not more) to say about the formality of its design as did the general historical development noted by, among others, Clement Eaton: "the style of gardens changed in the nineteenth century to fit the romantic temper of the period. Instead of regular formal walks, flower beds of geometric design, clipped hedges, and the prim, highly civilized look of the eighteenth century, Southern gardens and landscapes of the ante-bellum period took on informality, expressed in serpentine walks, irregular grouping of trees, and romantic vistas."[11] Placement of the house on the site is seldom without concern for the *vista*, the view of approach, which expresses more about the individuality of the dwelling than does its placement at the axial or centripetal center on the site plan. This same immanent vision of the world informed the

Figure 1-2. Topological Plantation—Pharsalia
(Based on Ulrich B. Phillips, Life and Labor in the Old South *[Boston: Little, Brown, 1929])*

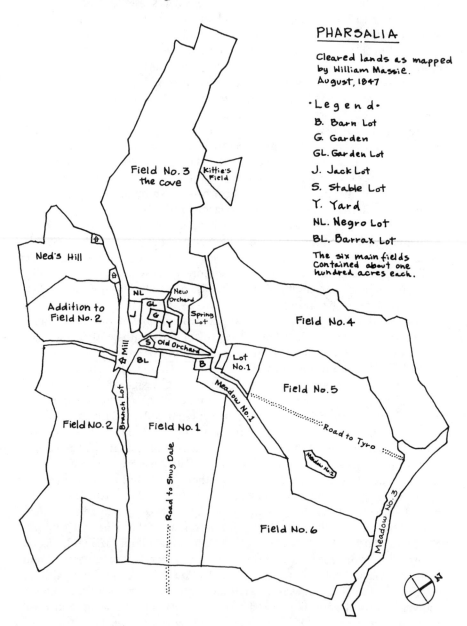

PHARSALIA

Cleared lands as mapped
by William Massie.
August, 1847

·Legend·

B. Barn Lot
G. Garden
GL. Garden Lot
J. Jack Lot
S. Stable Lot
Y. Yard
NL. Negro Lot
BL. Barrax Lot

The six main fields
contained about one
hundred acres each.

Field No. 3
the cove

Kitties
Field

Ned's Hill

Addition to
Field No. 2

NL

New
Orchard

GL

J   G
    Y

Spring
Lot

Field No. 4

Mill

S Old Orchard

BL

B

Lot
No. 1

Field No. 5

Branch Lot

Field No. 2

Field No. 1

Meadow No. 1

Road to Tyro

Meadow No. 2

Road to Snug Dale

Field No. 6

Meadow No. 3

N

Figure 1-3. Orthogonal Grid Plantation—Hopeton
(Based on Ulrich B. Phillips, Life and Labor in the Old South
[*Boston: Little, Brown, 1929*]*)*

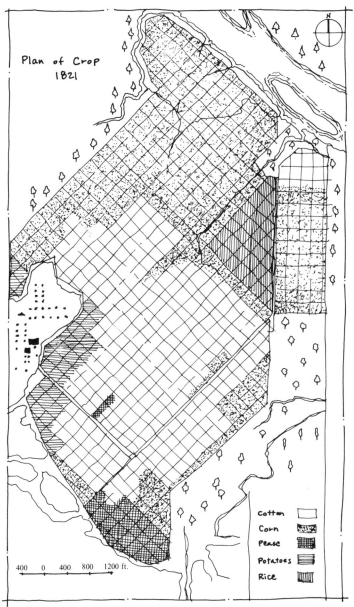

Plan of Crop
1821

Cotton
Corn
Pease
Potatoes
Rice

400   0   400   800   1200 ft.

MAP OF HOPETON ON THE ALTAMAHA

pre-Hellenistic Greek architect; the concern for how the structure is seen on its approach. The observations of Ida Thallon Hill and the theory of Konstantinos Doxiades argue the point that Greek architecture was based on visual perspective rather than on the geometrization of space. [12] The Greek architectural eye saw from within the space looking through and out of it. The Roman view was more axial, geometric, and symmetrical and saw the site from above, in plan; saw Rome at the center and all in symmetry around it. The Greeks, then, were, so to speak, more existential, the Romans ecumenical (imperial). To conceive an axially symmetrical view requires overview, a seeing-from-above, and indicates the conscious perception of one looking down. The perception of being in the environment concerned with one's actions and the world generates topological forms rather than geometrically symmetrical ones. As shall be seen in the legendary founding of Faulkner's fictional county seat of Jefferson, axially symmetrical planning is Roman. [13]

Finally, the propitious occurrence of Greek Revival style in the architectural history of the nation as a whole and of the South in particular must be placed in its appropriate context. As an outgrowth of the broader Neo-Classical spirit which possessed the country from about 1745 to 1830, it was fed by interest in the early excavations of Pompeii and Herculaneum, the subsequent publication of *Antiquities of Athens* in 1742, the interest of the Founding Fathers of Virginia in ancient Rome as a republic rather than a monarchy, [14] and in the contemporary Greek wars of independence, which became models for the American Revolution. [15] That part of the Georgian style of England that was accepted in the Colonies became the Georgian Colonial style from Pennsylvania northward, and what is loosely termed "Southern Colonial" through Virginia, Kentucky, Tennessee, and the Old Southwest. [16] The later and particular success of Greek Revival in the South is usually attributed to the advantages of the temple portico in mitigating the effects of the semitropical climate. [17] But this and even the historical factor of Greece's war of independence with Turkey in the 1820s were reasons subordinate to the larger one; that the temple form, in even so small a detail as a four-column prostyle portico, architecturally embodied the cultural communion of the South with the Attic world. [18] Not all building types can exhibit the cultural style, of course. Before addressing the architecture of Faulkner's novels, then, we might examine the well-known icon of the Southern way of life, the manor house.

The Southern public man not only built his house in the style of the great public buildings, as Vitruvius instructed him, [19] but built his country house in terms of what kind of life might be lived in it, as Palladio advised. [20] The result was a piece of expressive space, a concretization of the cultural milieu. Donald Davidson writes: "The South has always had a native architecture, adapted from classic models into something distinctly Southern; and nothing more

Figure 1-4.   Shadows-on-the-Teche Plantation (1830)
              Topologically-sited orthogonal house
              (Based on J. Frazer Smith, White Pillars: Early Life and Architecture of
              the Lower Mississippi Valley Country *[New York: Bramhall House,
              1941])*

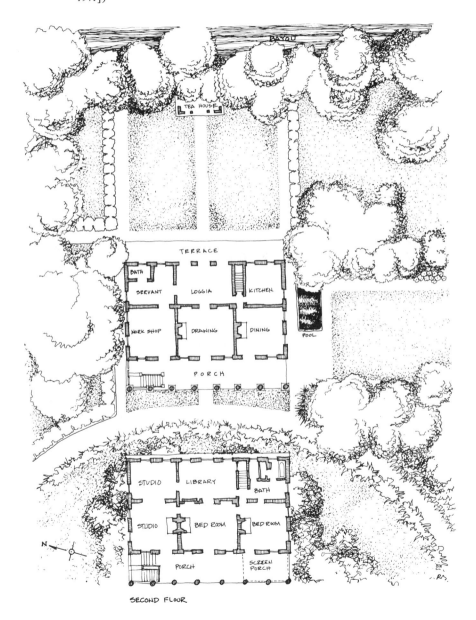

Figure 1-5. Malmaison Plantation (1845)
Axial site with asymmetrical addition
(Based on J. Frazer Smith, White Pillars: Early Life and Architecture of
the Lower Mississippi Valley Country [*New York: Bramhall House*,
1941]*)*

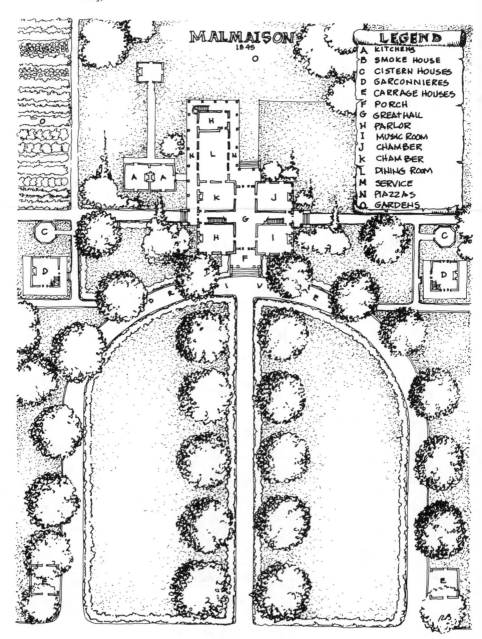

Figure 1-6. Uncle Sam Plantation (1840–50)
Plantation site with axial symmetry
(Based on J. Frazer Smith, White Pillars: Early Life and Architecture of
the Lower Mississippi Valley Country *[New York: Bramhall House,
1941])*

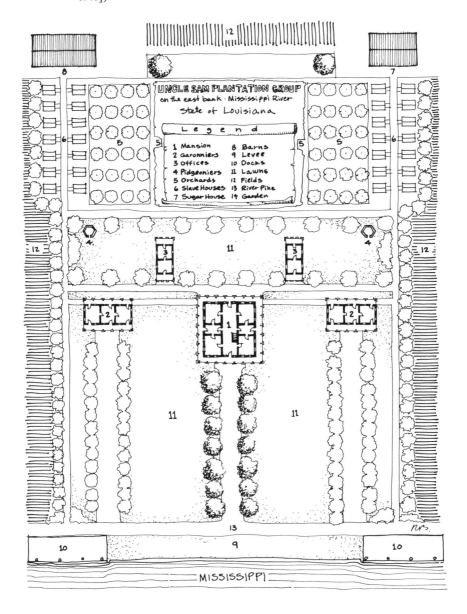

Figure 1-7. Evergreen Plantation (ca. 1840)
Strict orthogonal plantation site
(Based on J. Frazer Smith, White Pillars: Early Life and Architecture of
the Lower Mississippi Valley Country [*New York: Bramhall House,*
1941]*)*

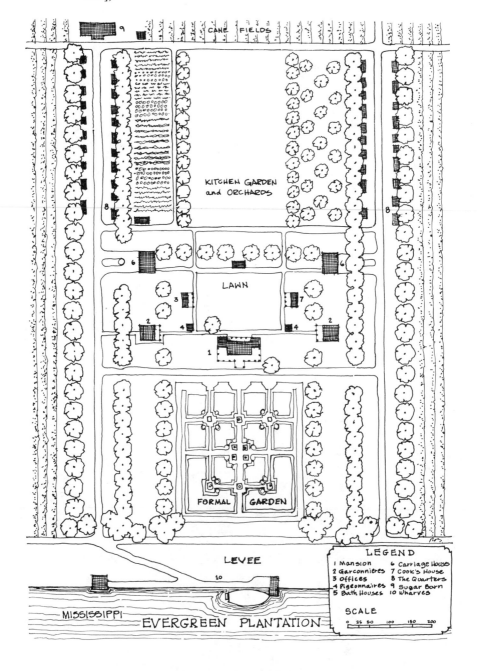

CANE FIELDS

KITCHEN GARDEN
and ORCHARDS

LAWN

FORMAL GARDEN

LEVEE

MISSISSIPPI

EVERGREEN PLANTATION

LEGEND
1 Mansion   6 Carriage House
2 Garconnières   7 Cook's House
3 Offices   8 The Quarters
4 Pigeonnaires   9 Sugar Barn
5 Bath Houses   10 Wharves

SCALE
0 25 50   100   150   200

clearly and satisfactorily belongs where it is, or better expresses the beauty and stability of an ordered life, than its old country homes, with their pillared porches, their simplicity of design, their sheltered groves, their walks bordered with boxwood shrubs."[21]

These words suggest both the Classical reference of the style and the central idea embodied in the mansion as a building type. As the Greek Revival style of the Southern mansion derives from the Classical affinity of its culture and the architectural moment, the building type is an architectural descendant of the English Georgian Colonial manor house. The political, social, and cultural beliefs of Georgian England, themselves derived from Classical sources, produced the manor house as a cultural institution, the embodiment of what was enduring, permanent, hereditary, traditional, noble, and valuable. This institution crossed the Atlantic with the First Families, generating the mansion form in this country as a continuance of the manor house tradition in England. Francis Pendelton Gaines remarks that travelers such as Eddis, Lyell and Van Buren noted the "similiarity in general structure between the Southern plantation and historic English manor"[22]; and cultural writers have noted that country estates in both the Old World and the New represented stability, order, permanence, and the settled attitude of an established society.[23] They also seemed to embody in their details certain attributes and virtues of the gentlemen patriarchs who inhabited them— virtues which had Classical referents through the Renaissance. These virtues were the active pursuit of leisure (which required a place of the proper character to encourage philosophic contemplation) and the virtue of hospitality, which is practiced in dwelling. Both leisure and hospitality, of course, are thought of and practiced as domestic amenities rather than public ones. Classical mention of hospitality can be found, appropriately enough, in the most fundamental of architectural treatises, Vitruvius's *Ten Books of Architecture*, in his discussion of the design of the Greek house.[24] Though the virtue, of course, consists in the actions of the host, the house itself becomes the intermediate object that concretizes the dweller's hospitality. The standard plan of the Greek house, with its central court, is more illustrative of the closed life of the family. But the Southern manor house in its time became, almost to the exclusion of all else, the concretization of hospitality in the nineteenth-century South.[25] The permanence, stability, and graciousness of plantation life in this country created, as it did in seventeenth-century England, a lyrically tempered literary form, often called the plantation novel.

To the extent that the image of the ideal life lived on the plantation was a descendant of life in the English country house, it may be said that the plantation novel has roots in the English manor house tradition in literature examined so thoroughly by Richard Gill in his *Happy Rural Seat*.[26] The tradition seeks to fix an image of plantation life as the good life, and to examine the trials of maintaining its values in the face of extreme chaos or change, war, or the breakup of the family.

In this country the plantation novel as a literary subgenre began as early as 1832 with the publication of John Pendleton Kennedy's *Swallow Barn* and was continued through the novels of William Gilmore Simms and John Esten Cooke. The tradition later survived its own excesses during the Romantic age, when the image was idealized to produce such pieces of the so-called Moonlight and Magnolia School as Thomas Nelson Page's *Red Rock*, and came to flower in works of the Southern literary renascence of the twentieth century, among them Stark Young's *So Red the Rose*, Eudora Welty's *Delta Wedding*, Allen Tate's *The Fathers,* and Andrew Lytle's *The Velvet Horn.*

Though the first significance of the mansion image in such novels is the stability and permanence of the society, there are other attendant complementary meanings. Each of these presents the concretization of a particular view of the world in both private and public station.[27] The house on the land as an ancestral seat came to express all the notions of family and attachment to the land implicit in Southern thinking. The Southern planter, as Richard Weaver says, "had a profound conviction that a family is not established until it belongs to a place, that a local habitation and a name go together."[28] The plantation manor house is above all the concrete expression of the station of the last Classical Christian gentleman, the Southern planter as aristocratic patriarch. Though there are certainly other building types in the fiction of William Faulkner (which this study will treat hereafter), one of the most vigorously symbolic architectural structures is the mansion of his paradigmatic patriarch, John Sartoris. It is this piece of fictive architecture to which we now turn.

2

The Unvanquished:
"The Aura of Father's Dream"

The Sartoris home is the archetype of the Southern manor house in the Yoknapatawpha canon. It has all the customary accoutrements and details and suffers all the legendary consequences of a house of its type in the South during the Civil War and after. In both *Sartoris* and *The Unvanquished* it is a domain and a center to which most of its inhabitants return again and again. Despite the fact that the novel *Sartoris* appeared some nine years before *The Unvanquished*, both the novels and their shared landscape should be studied in their narrative order. Faulkner certainly wrote *The Unvanquished* toward the story he had already given in *Sartoris*. The architectural consistency in both novels supports this view. And though the house is given more detailed description in *Sartoris*, a catalog of its features in *The Unvanquished* requires from the earlier novel reference only to how the house is sited on the land. Sartoris the *place* is four miles north of Jefferson,[1] and before the summer of 1863 its ensemble consists of a house, a stable and barn behind it, at least two Negro cabins, a smokehouse, an apple orchard, a pasture, and some bottom-land. The house itself has front and back galleries (*Unvanquished*, pp. 9, 22, 39), a central hall with rooms on either side, a stairway to an upper floor with four bedrooms, and four chimneys of two flues each, one for each of its eight fireplaces. The plan is presumed to be the standard H-plan or enclosed dog-trot arrangement. The house faces east (*Sartoris*, p. 8), the central hall running east to west, and the floor plan is fairly easy to decipher from the light, shade, and shadow patterns of sun and moon in both novels. The bedrooms are assuredly upstairs, according to the customary distinction of public and private areas. The kitchen, less public than the dining room, is certainly to the rear of the house at the northwest corner of the plan, and the dining room is at the northeast corner. But it is somewhat unusual for the kitchen to be attached and part of the plan here. In houses of this type the kitchen was usually detached from the main body of the house as a precaution against fire. Since the kitchen is not mentioned in "An Odor of Verbena," and the house as it appears in *Sartoris/Flags in the Dust* has such a kitchen, it must be assumed that after the war John rebuilt it as such, so that these two later houses are one and the same in parti and plan. As for the south half of the earlier plan, the "back parlor" must be the southwest room, leaving only the southeast corner for the office. In the standard plan for such houses, stairways are hung along one or the other walls of the hallway, usually beginning at mid-hall and ascending to the rear. The *antebellum* Sartoris house has a stairway which is rendered as straight (p. 19), from the top of which Bayard and Ringo can see the door of John's study or library, respectfully called "the Office" (p. 17). This doorway is visible from the top stair, regardless of which side of the hall supports the stairs.[2] Also, the Office is a bit more public than either the dining room or kitchen and so is more probably a front room of the house. The propriety of the names for this room is fairly evident to the reader. John calls it "the Office" because he conducts the business of the place there, even the business of the family, as when Bayard goes to tell his father he has kissed Drusilla (p. 264). The Negroes call it the Office "because into this room they would be fetched to face the Patroller..."(pp. 17–18). The modern equivalent is to be "called on the carpet." Rosa Millard calls the same room "the Library" both because John's bookcase of wisdom is there and because her felt necessity is to emphasize the values of the household over its business.[3]

Another important point is that the architectural plans of *antebellum* Sartoris are not nearly as decipherable as *post*-1870 Sartoris, because there is less description of the *antebellum* house in *The Unvanquished*. Beyond the lack of detail and the mythical tenor of *The Unvanquished*, the more significant reason for the uncertain plan here is that young Bayard is not nearly as aware of his place and its physical architectural layout as he is later in *Sartoris* or even in "An Odor of Verbena," although he is probably unconsciously aware of it and half consciously descriptive of it as narrator.

Sartoris also has an attic, which plays a more significant role in the novel *Sartoris* as the room which contains many of the *things* of the family and the house. Attics are the repository of the valued things of the past. These things are nearly always kept in trunks in the attic, unless they are the furniture of the past. Sartoris has an attic with several trunks, one of which has a specific use in *The Unvanquished*. It is taken down from the attic to have the silver service and silverware put in it (pp. 15–16) before it is buried. It is later taken out of the ground and put in Rosa's room before the aborted trip to Memphis. The trunk contains the heritage of the past embodied in the family's silver, and Rosa hides the trunk behind her bed (p. 47) as she hides the boys in her skirts (p. 31). Most of these objects are not mentioned until after the house is burnt and only parts of them remain. Among the most significant are John's desk, an old rifle hung above the mantel, a big clock, a dining table at which John has "his old place" (p. 13), a hearth, the trunks in the attic, and outside, some flowers which must be tended, and gates (*Unvanquished*, p. 51, *Sartoris*, p. 6) which are later "broken clean off" (*Unvanquished*, p. 90). *Sartoris* also has earth, and whatever the complexity of the architectural detail in *The Unvanquished* and throughout *Sartoris*, the explication of the imaginative spaces here might begin with the small patch of dirt where Bayard and Ringo have constructed nothing less than a model landscape of their entire known world: western Mississippi from Jefferson to Vicksburg.

The Unvanquished, like *As I Lay Dying*, is a novel of motion and movement. It is a novel of topology, maps and landscapes and of paths between places, where the paths and the traversing of them are more important than the places to which they lead. Sartoris, Hawkhurst, Vicksburg, and Corinth are places to Bayard and Ringo, but so is Tennessee. Colonel John is repeatedly said to be *at* Tennessee, as he would be *at* Corinth (p. 7). The living map that Ringo and Bayard create in the dirt behind the smokehouse is at once an architectural model and an historical document.[4] Here earth is the medium for concretizing the events of history, and when the boys travel to Hawkhurst, Bayard brings some of the Sartoris earth with him—"enough to last" (p. 63). The significance of the soil is explicit in the novel. Bayard records that "it was more than Sartoris earth; it was Vicksburg too: the yelling was in it, the embattled, the iron-worn, the supremely invincible" (p. 62). The earth here is the substance of the homeland defended. Even the living map in the dirt has "that ponderable though passive recalcitrance of topography which outweighs artillery..."(p. 3). It is the substance of the *genius loci* of the land and contains the fury of its defense against other invading spirits. Bayard had to bring enough earth to continually concretize the *genius loci* of his homeland until the war was over. Like Stark Young's Edward McGehee, he knows that the future of his family and of the South "goes with the land."[5]

The importance of Sartoris the place—the importance of the house on its site—is revealed within the rather complex working of dreams in the novel. Dreams are of two kinds in *The Unvanquished:* dreams of events and dreams of aspiration. The dreams which Rosa and young Bayard have—of Loosh disclosing the whereabouts of the buried trunk of silver and of the destruction of the house—are dreams of coming events. They are dreams which become reality and in Bayard's case are the reverse of certain other events where reality appears as a dream. The silver service removed from the sideboard (p. 16) and placed in the trunk is one of the Sartoris *lares* and *penates*, a thing of value to be saved from destruction. When Bayard dreams of the loss of the house "it was like I was looking at our place and suddenly the house and stable and cabins and trees and all were gone and I was looking at a place flat and empty as the sideboard..." (p. 27). The simile emphasizes the point: the place which is home without its built structures, its architectural concretizations of meaning, is as vacant of meaning as the sideboard without its heirloom silver service. It is an altar without a chalice, a flat space dangerously devoid of meaningful forms. When Bayard wakes from his dream, the danger is imminent; a mounted Union soldier stands a few yards away, looking at the house through field glasses. The image of the house on the land is a value nearly unto itself. It is a vision to Bayard as he and Ringo run toward the house after shooting at the Union rider: "The house didn't seem to get any nearer; it just hung there in front of us, floating and increasing slowly in size, like something in a dream..." (p. 30). Here, and indeed throughout *The Unvanquished,* dream and reality are reversed. Bayard dreams what will eventually become real, while the real appears as a dream. Later in the novel, after the house has been burnt, Ringo sets the image of the house on paper as he looks at the ruins. The Union lieutenant watching him sees that Ringo draws it "like it used to be," to which Ringo answers, " 'What I wanter draw hit like hit is now?' " (p. 160). What Ringo would rather look at is a picture of the once-living house, a vision of order retained from the past by his memory. The image retains much more than the rendering shows because it contains the experience of dwelling within it, which Ringo knows and the lieutenant does not.[6] Hence the ruins have more significance to the lieutenant than the house as it was, and the picture means more to Ringo than the ruins.

When John later rebuilds the house, he actualizes a dream of aspiration which, after the war, replaces the dream of event. The dream of aspiration is of a kind such as the founders of Jefferson hold as a community in *Requiem for a Nun.* The Jefferson courthouse is the concretization of the dream, the "repository of the aspirations and the hopes" the community holds for its future (*Requiem,* p. 40). The dream of aspiration is in many ways the opposite of the dream of event; it is a hope wished for and acted upon. The dream of event is passive; it is hoped *against* and happens *to* the world.

Both kinds of dreams are realized in terms of the fictive architecture of *The Unvanquished.* The dreams of event are of the destruction of the house and the disclosure of the buried trunk of silver. John's dream of aspiration includes the rebuilding of his house, the rebuilding of his community, and the reestablishment of his place within it. It is part of his patriarchal station, and to build a house with the intention of concretizing one's existential station is the essential act of creating meaningful place. As such his dream contrasts with Thomas Sutpen's.

Sartoris is often compared to Sutpen in both the fiction and its criticism, for they represent the best and the worst of their kind, the dream and its opposite, the design. Bayard's characterization of Sutpen in *The Unvanquished* is illustrative: "He was underbred, a cold ruthless man who had come into the country about thirty years before the War, nobody knew from where except Father said you could look at him and know he would not dare to tell. He had got some land and nobody knew how he did that either, and got money from somewhere ... and built a big house and married and set up as a gentleman" (p. 255).

It is certainly an indication of contrivance to "set up as a gentleman," for Sutpen has not the imagination to dream, only the cold cunning to carry out a "design," according to what he refers to as his "schedule." His conception of suzerainty has no outside purpose, is not concerned with the public affirmation of a traditional pattern for living the best life possible. His plan is thus a private one, more concerned with the appearance of respectability than adherence to the right order. With the coming of the Civil War, Sutpen and Sartoris both assume duties of leadership, though for Sutpen the war constitutes a threat more to his design than to the community of which he is part. After 1865, Sartoris is still tending to his duties of patriarchal tenure. His dispatch of the two Burden carpetbaggers and ousting of their candidate Cassius Benbow is a *dokimasia*.[7] His return of the ballot box to his home is not only an attempt to bring government under his sphere of order; his domain is a place of retreat and a surrogate habitation for the threatened political order. And when Sartoris organizes a group of nightriders to prevent the carpetbaggers from inciting insurrection, Sutpen will not be involved. To Colonel John's appeal he answers, "I'm for my land. If every man of you would rehabilitate his own land, the country would take care of itself" (p. 256). He has come back to restore his private dream. "But his dream is just Sutpen," Drusilla tells Bayard, "John's is not. He is thinking of this whole country which he is trying to raise by its bootstraps ... " (p. 256). To raise one's self by one's bootstraps is usually a reflexive verb. But here John is raising the "whole country"—the community, himself included—by *its* bootstraps. He raises the community by helping to lead it, and raises himself in the process. The public part of the dream is first in the mind of John Sartoris, and the conclusion is just as important. As long as the dream remains somewhat public and community-minded, the aspirations remain wholesome and the architecture vital. When private aspirations are intentionalized by those with public responsibilities, the dream is but a design and the architecture a rotting shell, like Sutpen's Hundred.

John's militant performance of his communal office is part of his rebuilding of the town. "They were building Jefferson back, the courthouse and the stores," writes Bayard, and it is significant that Bayard, Drusilla, and Joby are in the log yard cutting cypress and oak into planks to rebuild the house while John is building the town. As builder he is the one who does his home too, and by 1870 he has succeeded in building what Drusilla knows as the objectification of the *idea* Sartoris: "And father had rebuilt the house too, on the same blackened spot, over the same cellar, where the other had burned, only larger, much larger: Drusilla said that the house was the aura of Father's dream just as a bride's trousseau and veil is the aura of hers" (p. 253). The house is not the concretization of the dream, however, but the aura of the dream, and to clarify this something must be said of the phenomenology of *aurae*. They are related in their own way in this novel to both dreams and concretized space.

An *aura* is a distinctive atmosphere, often luminous, from a specific source, a kind of "shining forth" of person or object. It is nearly synonymous with a *nimbus*, the aura of a sacred person or thing, but an aura is secular. It may be thought of as uncontained or unstructured meaningful space.

A person or thing, a house or an object emits an aura. But in *The Unvanquished* and in Drusilla's thought, the dream emits the aura, and the house is the concretization of the aura and the embodiment of the dream. The dream shines forth in the aura and the house is the aura contained, enclosed. Since the aura is like an atmosphere, to live in the house is to live not in the dream, but in the aura of the dream—to live in a structure which contains the atmosphere of the aspiration. Thus there is nothing abstract or ethereal here, only imperceptible, just as the air which makes life possible is still a real substance. To live in a dream would be the abstraction. The *genius loci* of the dwelling which concretizes it is thus just as real as is atmosphere, and just as difficult to feel with the senses.

To rebuild the house is to reaffirm the dream; an established relationship of order and continuity, an awareness of contingency, and a sense of purposeful existence. The house bodies forth the dream in the way that Drusilla's simile suggests. The bride's trousseau and veil are at once the container of the person they define and the expression of the station of bridehood she holds. The Sartoris house is the physical guise and container of the family's character and the concretization of John's place in the world. Its rebuilding signifies the return of order to the community through the return of order to the landscape.

The narrative action of *The Unvanquished* is driven by its objects and paths. The view is most often of objects on the landscape, seen while in motion down a path, things passed *on the way* to one place or another. The novel involves its people in a vertical hierarchy and the environment in a horizontal process. The hierarchy is the common ontological hierarchy of man, animal, plant, and mineral or thing. The process is the Civil War, moving through the landscape as an incendiary force; and men move closer to the plane of the landscape and down and up the chain of being according to the demands and circumstances thrust on them by the fire of war. The war occurs as fire especially to the built environment of courthouse, town square, mansion, and cabin, where it renders the human landscape into a surrogate mechanical landscape.[8] Whatever the burning war attacks, whether artifact or architecture, its effect is to consume the animate, natural, or human part and leave behind only the functional, mechanical, metal parts. When the Sartoris house is burned, the four chimneys are all that remain; and the only things recovered from the ashes are the iron barrel and mechanism of the musket John kept above the parlor mantel (pp. 88–89) and the insides, that is, the mechanical parts, of the big clock. The parts that involve human craftsmanship and skill, meaning and value, are destroyed; the humanistic is burned away, as the war reduces all art to logic and all metaphysics to physics, the rigid iron rules of existence.[9] What Ringo retains from the Union horse he and Bayard shot in the beginning of the novel is a saddle buckle (p. 62), and at one point the Union army is spotted by the flicker of its guns and bits (p. 159).

The built environment beyond the Sartoris home endures the same effects. A wagon accosted by troops has its animate parts—its mules—removed. At Hawkhurst, which is by now a chimneyed ash pile too, Bayard and Ringo discover that Union troops have burnt the railroad ties and left the rails twisted around the trees. Some structures of the neutral landscape in *The Unvanquished* become part of the mechanical environment, like the railroad, the cotton gins, and the infamous cotton compress where Rosa Millard is murdered. Little can be said of lesser structures like Ab Snopes's cabin or the cotton gins. But the abandoned cotton compress as a place has appropriate affiliations with the events which happen there. As a place where cotton is compacted into tighter bails for distant shipment, its function is more mechanical and less humanly controlled than a gin, and has closer connections to the railroad.

The railroad in Faulkner is the quintessential machine in the garden,[10] especially in the hunting stories of *Go Down, Moses*. But here it is an agent of the war, with an absolute linearity to its method, and a fire inside. It is the singular symbol of the fire and fever which infects both landscape and men and of which John cannot cure himself after the war. It is the same fire which Faulkner, in the historical account in *Requiem for a Nun*, calls "the iron and fire of civilization" (p. 257), though in this later novel he had come to see a positive effect of its sweep over Jefferson: "The town was as though insulated by fire or perhaps cauterised by fire from fury and turmoil" (p. 232).

Objects in the hand are the smallest scale of fictive architecture, and during the war objects carried in the hand carry fire. After shooting at the Yankee, Bayard and Ringo carry the old musket "like a log" (p. 29), something which at least potentially carries fire. The Yankee who rides around the Sartoris house to catch John in the barn carries a short carbine "in one hand like a lamp" (p. 82). The lamp is the domestic tool to carry domesticated fire. The carbine is a wartime mechanical tool to carry wartime fire. And later, as Bayard stands before his grandmother's murderer, the gun in his hand feels "heavy as a firedog" (p. 207), as ponderous as the iron grating which holds the household fire.

John carries the fire in a hand-held object rigged with mechanical remnants; a derringer "held flat inside his left wrist by a clip he made himself of wire and an old clock spring" (p. 268). The larger symbol, the railroad, John takes to building again after the war, and its linearity and momentum carry him to his end. After quoting George Wyatt's succinct statement of John's flaw ("'I know what's wrong: he's had to kill too many folks, and that's bad for a man'"), Bayard recalls that his father "had stepped straight from the pilot of that engine into the race for the legislature" (p. 260), after which Redmond kills him.

Infection with fire and the mechanism of war is the particular malady of John Sartoris. The characters of "Vendée" are involved in a very different way with the hierarchy of being, the singularly remarkable aspect of which is the verticality of its arrangement on the landscape. Its highest station is that of a man on horseback; below it are stances and postures closer to the ground and directly representative of more elemental pursuits. The more basic and fundamental the values fought for, the closer the protagonist is found to the earth. It may be useful here to speak of an animal landscape and a plant and inanimate landscape. Both are, of course, contained within one another, but the descent of a man from his mount, while bringing him in direct contact with the earth, often has to do with the elemental pursuit of justice or with the simple condition of survival. The animal landscape is the level of snakes, mules and horses, and men within it are on horseback.

Beyond and below this level is a plant and inanimate landscape, to which men totally revert when enacting the business of Themistic justice. It is a landscape of bushes and trees, clearings and mud. Men are dismounted here. *They* are the animals.

The articulation of these levels begins as Grumby becomes involved in Rosa Millard's mule trading. His renegades terrorize the countryside so that "the Negroes who had lost their white people lived hidden in caves back in the hills like animals" (p. 171). When Rosa goes to find Grumby in the old cotton compress, the road into the bottom where Bayard and Ringo wait in the wagon "looked like a cave" (p. 173). When they go to encounter the act which precipitates their vendée they step down and leave the wagon to run "in the ankle-deep mud of that old road" (p. 175). Though the room where the old woman lies is "raised about two feet from the earth," Bayard ends up on his hands and knees before the body of his beloved grandmother. He now begins a long pursuit on horseback, for the purpose of literally running Grumby to earth.

During the long hunt, when Matt Bowden visits Buck and Bayard's camp to lead them off the trail of Grumby and his riders, he dismounts but does not hitch, keeping in touch with his mount. Later, when he and Bridges hand Grumby over to Bayard, first one and then the other mounts his horse; they neither have nor want any part in the business between Grumby and Bayard. And as they ride off, Bayard and Ringo dismount, Bayard not even remembering when nor why, "but we were down" (p. 207). The stage is now set for the final confrontation.

Up to now Grumby and his gang have been associated with snakes—first with the half-frozen water moccasin Ringo finds, then by Buck's reference to the compress as a snake den, and finally by Ab Snopes's calling them a passel of rattlesnakes. Shortly afterwards, Bayard suggests that Grumby looks like a bear, then follows with what is, in this hierarchy, the worst of insults: "he seemed more like a stump than even an animal" (p. 209). The comparisons are obviously in descending, deteriorating order. Grumby is thought of not even as animal but as tree, and a dead piece of tree at that. When the raider fires and misses Bayard and the groveling fight in the mud begins, the participants imitate animals; Ringo leaps on Grumby "looking exactly like a frog, even to the eyes," and Grumby in turn "buck[s] Ringo off just like a steer would" (p. 120).

During this fundamental struggle between Bayard and his antagonist, the smells that he senses from Grumby are a review of the complete hierarchy, in perfect order: "I could smell him—the smell of man's sweat, and the gray coat grinding into my face and smelling of horse sweat and wood smoke and grease" (p. 209). The odors run from human to animal to vegetative wood, to inanimate smoke and finally to less than inanimate, the grease of mechanical things.

Finally, Bayard has at least two opportunities, before the fight and after, to raise Uncle Buck's gun on Grumby. At first the weapon feels too heavy, "heavy as a firedog in my hand" (p. 209). A firedog has meaningful domestic associations, even though it is the mechanical part of the hearth. When the final task comes—shooting Grumby as he runs away—the gun is compared to something less associative, less personal, and yet somehow natural. To Bayard it feels "steady as a rock" (p. 210); it is like a stone, part of the inanimate landscape, the most impersonal and perhaps the most natural, certainly the most inevitable thing on earth.

After the deed is done, Bayard and Ringo return from the natural to the human landscape, the built environment of Jefferson, "the sooty walls that hadn't fallen down yet" (p. 211). The last analogy for Grumby is Uncle Buck's vision of his body "pegged out on the door to [the compress] like a coon hide" (p. 213), the animal rendered inanimate.

These landscapes and the characteristics men assume from them do not go away with the end of the war. As said before, John cannot change his ways and continues to fight for his dream in the old manner. The characteristics appear again in "An Odor of Verbena," in Bayard's recollection of his father's eyes, "which in the last two years had acquired that transparent film which the eyes of carnivorous animals have" (p. 266); in the "vulture-like formality" in the faces of the men who have waited for Bayard's return; in Drusilla's voracity; and even in Bayard himself, who pants in grief instead of crying.

When Bayard faces his father's bane, he confronts Redmond upstairs in his office instead of down on the ground, but it is noted that Redmond holds his pistol in a "rocklike hand" (p. 286). Yet as the fire has left the landscape and the town has been rebuilt, there is no fever in Bayard's work as he rebuilds the Sartoris tradition without undue violence.

3

Sartoris:
"Time and Its Furniture"

The later life of Bayard Sartoris is in many ways more interior, as is the fictive architecture of *Sartoris*, with quite different levels than *The Unvanquished*. The Civil War novel is set on the land, where the levels of landscape and the house on its site are important. Though paths and places are present in *Sartoris*, its chief architectural element is the room, after which come roads and places, especially the *old* places.

The Sartoris home is the same in both novels, and the plans are nearly identical, with some variance in room arrangement. The house of 1919 has a detached though undefined kitchen,[1] and the northwest room is no longer the kitchen but the dining room. The northeast room is the parlor in both *Sartoris* and in the rebuilt house of *The Unvanquished*. The conjectured plan takes Bayard's description literally—that John has rebuilt the house "on the same blackened spot, over the same cellar, where the other had burned, only larger, much larger" (*Unvanquished*, p. 253). The "same cellar" indicates that the same footings and foundation are used, which together with the remaining four chimneys of the house, would necessitate the same overall dimensions. The house is "much larger" then because the dining room of the earlier plan is now at the rear, the kitchen is rebuilt detached, and what was the dining room is now a more contemporary room, the parlor.[2] There are other new details in "An Odor of Verbena," such as a portico and columns instead of a gallery (p. 267), a garden and flower beds (pp. 251, 253, 254), chandeliers (p. 267), and colored glass from the original Sartoris Carolina house, now set in a fanlight in the western window of the drawing room (p. 271, 291).[3] In *Sartoris* this glass is set in windows at the east end of the upstairs hall, and the south half of the plan is reversed. The drawing room is in front, and Old Bayard's library/office is at the rear. The differing arrangement indicates old Bayard's semiretired station, for which his office is more of a library, given more to the contemplation of stored wisdom than the active business of either law or banking. In such a house, the drawing room has a more public function as a place of hospitality, and is less a place for the musings of an old patriarch.[4]

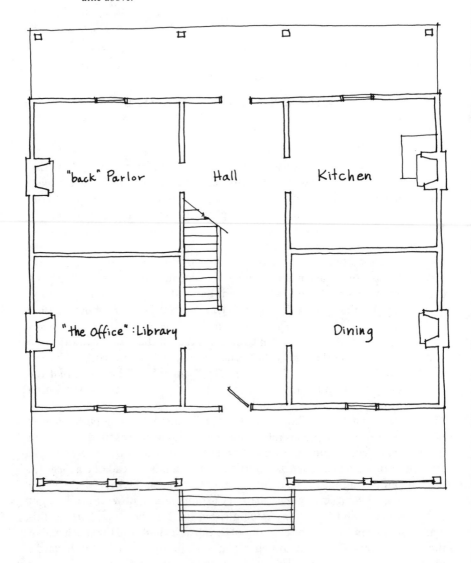

Figure 3-1. First Floor Plan as in *The Unvanquished* (until Summer 1963)
Second floor rooms unspecified: Bayard and Ringo's room
(*Unvanquished*, p. 19), Rosa's room (*Unvanquished*, pp. 46–47), and the
attic above.

"back" Parlor Hall Kitchen

"the Office": Library Dining

Figure 3-2. Second Floor Plan as in *The Unvanquished* (after 1870)

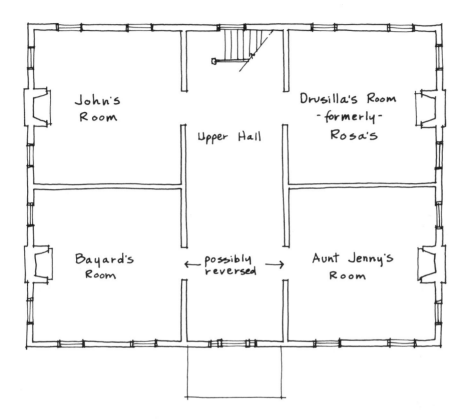

Bayard's office is one of at least four rooms in *Sartoris* which Faulkner describes in some detail, and each of these is a space with character and significance enough to look at individually. They embody the character of old Bayard, the ghosts of his family's past and the history of the family itself. Together they not only concretize the Sartoris *genius loci* but illustrate the process of how a living past bodies forth its meaning within a house.

The description of Bayard's office centers on the object which makes it a library: his bounteous bookcase. The first volumes mentioned are those of Bayard's law profession, the "heavy legal tomes bound in dun calf" (p. 34). Yet their presence suggests meditation, not the practice of law, and their mention is quickly followed by notice of Bayard's principal current reading, his Dumas, of which "one volume lay always on the night-table beside his bed" (p. 34).

Figure 3-3.   First Floor Plan as in *The Unvanquished* (after 1870) and Second Floor
Plan as in *Sartoris/Flags in the Dust*

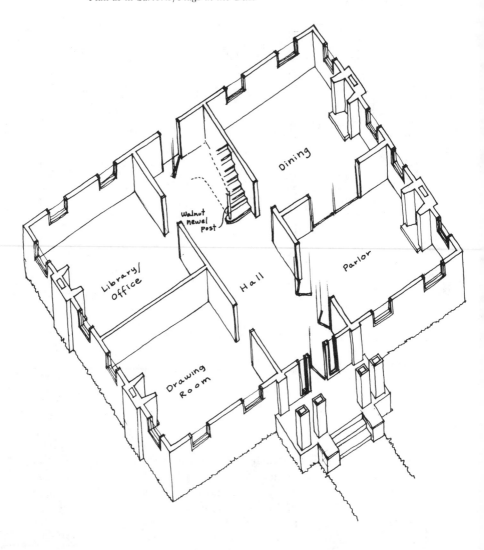

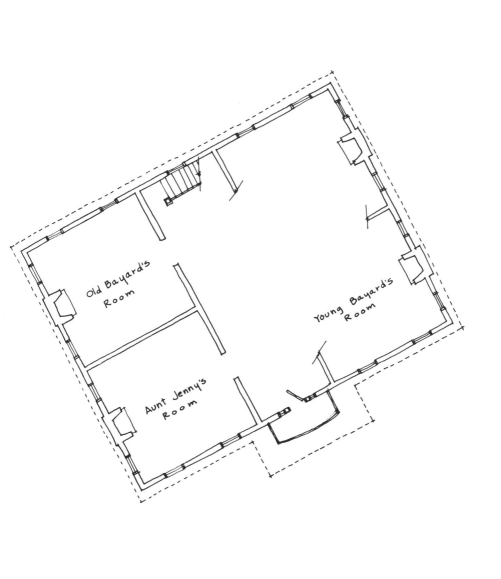

Old Bayard's Room

Aunt Jenny's Room

Young Bayard's Room

Figure 3-4. Site Plan as in *Sartoris*/*Flags in the Dust*

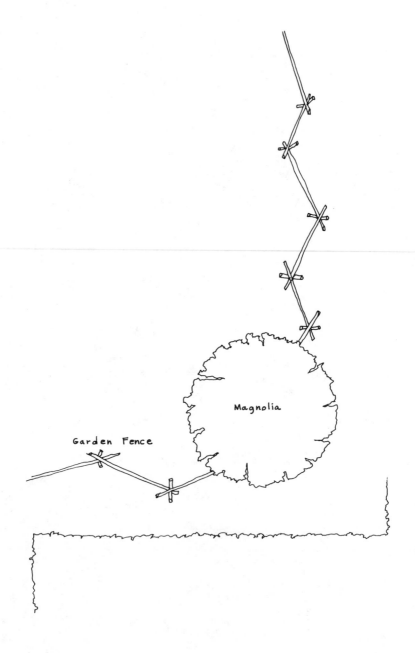

Magnolia

Garden Fence

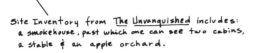

Site Inventory from <u>The Unvanquished</u> includes:
a smokehouse, past which one can see two cabins,
a stable & an apple orchard.

Kitchen

. detached
but undefined

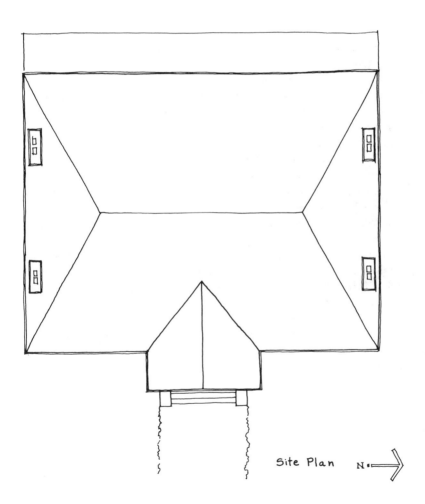

Site Plan   N →

The rest of the objects on the bookcases, a curious collection of seeds, roots, grain pods, "old rusted spurs and bits and harness buckles" (p. 34), denote old Bayard as neither lawyer nor banker nor gallant soldier like his father but as gentleman farmer, and certainly the times have not demanded more.[5] This room is a match for his office at the bank, which also has another ostensibly official use as the directors' room (p. 79). Here too Bayard's desk is a place of leisure over labor, and "like the one at home, was cluttered with a variety of objects which bore no relation whatever to the banking business, and the mantel above the fireplace bore still more objects of an agricultural nature" (p. 79). Dr. Peabody's office is the obvious comparative, with its clutter of paper, garments, bottles, lamp, axel grease and "various instruments pertaining to the occupant's profession" (p. 102). As a character descriptive, the room not only links these two gentlemen in temperament but anticipates Bayard's trust in the tempered medical wisdom of his friend.[6] As with the middle life of Isaac McCaslin, the reader is never told of the many years Bayard spent settled in his place as gentleman farmer pursuing the everyday business of his station. There is only this image of him at home, reclining among the cast-off bits of earth and seed which are part of his past peaceful existence.

Within these rooms are ghosts among the objects. Colonel John's ghost inhabits the pipe which old man Falls gives Bayard, a ghost "to be evoked like a genie or a deity . . . by a charred pipe from which even the rank smell of burnt tobacco had long since faded away" (p. 23).[7]

The ghost also inhabits the most formal room of the Sartoris house, the parlor. Its past reflects the reversals of the entire household. Before John's death "it had been constantly in use" (p. 59); now it is used "formally not at all" (p. 60). In the minds of the boys "the room was associated with death" and its shrouded furniture contributes to its mausoleum atmosphere. It is in the things of the room, the furniture and hearth, that the ghost of John Sartoris resides, and it took up residence the night of his wake, "contemplating for the last time his own apotheosis from the jocund mellowness of his generous hearth" (p. 59). His spirit becomes the fire of his own hearth, from which the hospitality of his home emanates.

As old Bayard's library is linked to his bank office, the parlor which Colonel John's ghost inhabits is closely associated with the other important room at Sartoris, the attic. But before old Bayard visits the attic, which contains other ghosts and objects, there occurs a particularly helpful metaphor. In Narcissa's musing remembrance of young Bayard's twin brother, John is definitively recalled as one "who had not waited for Time and its furniture to teach him that the end of wisdom is to dream high enough not to lose the dream in the seeking of it" (p. 74).

The first assumption would seem to be the correct one; namely, that Time is a *room*, or rather, that Time is *as* a room, having furniture which teaches the ends of wisdom. Time's furniture is not a difficult vehicle to grasp metaphorically; all phenomena seem to have the proper equipment to carry out their purposes. But Time is difficult to imagine as a room. Since the vehicle of any metaphor has only hypothetical status at best, Time is not a fictive room here, but rather something *like* a room; an enclosed space, or rather, the space within an enclosure, space with a particular character or nature. The word *aura* may be used judiciously here to denote a specific space which concretizes a humanly experienced phenomenon. Time is a kind of room; or better, time is an enclosed space with a particular aura,[8] having or possessing the furniture, the particular objects to articulate its aura, its character. We speak of the *sense* of time, the feeling of time passing, the *aura* of time. Faulkner's rooms, fictive or metaphorical, are spaces moved in and out of. The metaphorical ones depict time as a space of condition, an enclosed aura in which something happens. Faulkner's conception of time, then, is that of an experienced inhabited space, for which the architectonic idea of *room* is a useful metaphor. The further conclusion to be drawn from this understanding is *not* that what a room *is* may be as abstract as the concept of Time, but that Time is as concrete an experience as is a room, and conversely, that a room is as penetrating, infusing and circumambient an aura as is time. Men dwell in rooms as they dwell in time. In both cases, metaphorical and fictive, rooms concretize dreams, visions or memories. In *Requiem for a Nun*, the courthouse embodies the aspirations, the hopes and the dreams of the community. In *The Unvanquished*, John's house articulates his dream. In *Sartoris*, Time, like a room, teaches the nature of dream wisdom. The aura of time and the furniture which articulates it make up a room in which young John had never been (or at best had been in only briefly, certainly not long enough to teach him the end of wisdom). The exemplar for such dreaming is, again, Colonel John. The aura of his dream is an entire house and all its furniture. Time has indeed taught him not to dream too high. The furniture which keeps him mindful of this is all about his house, and the aura is but part of the furniture. *The Unvanquished* depicts the Colonel's actions in defense of his family and community during and after the war, his desperate attempt not to lose the dream in the seeking of it.[9] Young Bayard, in running Redmond out of town rather than shooting him, gives witness to the wisdom taught him by his father's aura and its furniture. The repository of this wisdom is the trunk which Old Bayard visits in his climb to the attic in *Sartoris*. It is a fingering of that furniture of time which teaches the wisdom of his ancestor.

Old Bayard's attic is thus a complement to the metaphor of "Time and its furniture." It is another room-aura with furniture. Bayard draws a chair up to the old cedar chest; he has brought light and some comfort to one corner of this room, and for a little while he will *dwell* there, in the aura of the past, surrounded by Time and its furniture.

That a man who so loves the past has not opened this trunk in eighteen years is curious. But it may well be so, since the pain of his son's death in 1901 may have kept him from returning in 1918 to note his grandson's death. Bayard usually visits the chest on the occasion of a death in his family. This time he visits it to place his father's pipe in the chest and to record the passing of three family members: his grandson John in July of the year before, and young Bayard's wife and son in October of the same year.

Bayard's visit to the cedar chest is similar to a visit to the grave (for instance, the walk to the grave in Allen Tate's "Ode to the Confederate Dead"). It is a sacramental visit to a time enclosure, performed with a number of sacred objects and with the infrequency of the last sacraments.

The *temporal* point to be made here is that old Bayard does *not* travel backward through time and history as he goes through the trunk. The objects here are more nearly in forward historical order as he comes upon them: garment, then rapier and sheath, then saber, pistols and derringer, army hat, pottery and machete, then back again in time to oil can and Confederate coat.

Little pattern can be drawn from this collection of objects. The rapier is obviously from the Carolina Sartoris and predates Colonel John's westward move to Mississippi in the 1830s. It lies here with John's Civil War arsenal, and the order of appearance—from rapier to saber to pistols to derringer—is obviously from the flamboyant to the utilitarian. All are the memorabilia of legends told thus far in the novel—the bravado of the Carolina Sartorises, John's service in the War, and his expulsion of the carpetbaggers thereafter. The forage-cap, vessel, and machete suggest that John served in the Mexican War, after he moved to Mississippi but before the Civil War. This part of John's life is without detail or legend throughout the Yoknapatawpha canon. The occurrence of these objects out of historical order is the puzzle. If the machete is part of the list of weapons it is appropriately last, less than utilitarian, *arma bruta.* Otherwise the Mexican items belong historically between the rapier and the saber.

The oil can, dated 1873, picks up the historical progression, but the coat and gown turn back again to the 1860s. The packet of yellowed papers and the Bible are trans-temporal, but the family record in the flyleaves is a documentation of its passing. What old Bayard encounters here is a collection of objects and a list of people which render a span of family history and give it form and meaning. The names at the top of the flyleaf are faded because the people are not important for where or who they came from but for what they have done, which is the point of the words that old Bayard recalls his father saying. The place for these reminiscences is precisely where Bayard is, the attic of memory.

Bayard has one thing to add to the chest—his father's pipe—and he places it, again, with Colonel John's other implements of fire, the dueling pistols. Whether the pipe is more or less flamboyant than the other objects, placing it with the pistols is also historically accurate.

There is another chest at Sartoris in the closet of the boys' room, to which Bayard stumbles after his first accident with the car. Young Bayard's addressing of this object is an obvious yet interesting counterpoint to old Bayard's approach to the trunk in the attic. The chest is a younger version of the trunk. It contains the same sort of objects—a garment, a book, and a piece of ordnance—but the differences are telling. The book is the New Testament, the newer part of the Bible, the younger half. The garment is a canvas hunting-coat, and together with the shotgun shell and the withered bear's paw, it attributes to young John the knowledge of, if not the wilderness, at least the values of the hunt.

Young Bayard, however, has nothing to add to these artifacts. Instead of keeping, preserving, or increasing them, he carries them outside and destroys them with fire. The blaze is made from the ashes of a washtub fire, a fire used to preserve other garments.

There are not only other houses but other kinds of houses in *Sartoris* which are, as pieces of fictive architecture, representative in varying ways. Sartoris is a typically ordered plan in the classical style and as such represents traditional society, order, permanence, and stability. It is the house as significant object. The Benbow house is representative by its siting and to a lesser extent by the character of its landscape architecture. It is set in the older, more "spacious and quiet" outskirts of Jefferson. By the time the house appears in the novel, a contrast has already been established between the Sartoris country house and the townhouse of Belle Mitchell.

The key to these in-town structures is their proximity to the street. Belle's is

a huge brick house set well up to the street. The lot had been the site of a fine old colonial house which stood among magnolias and oaks and flowering shrubs. But the house had burned, and some of the trees had been felled to make room for an architectural garbling so imposingly terrific as to possess a kind of majesty. It was a monument to the frugality (and the mausoleum of the social aspirations of his women) of a hill-man who had moved in from a small settlement called Frenchman's Bend and who, as Miss Jenny Du Pre put it, had built the handsomest house in Frenchman's Bend on the most beautiful lot in Jefferson....

The hill-man had built his house so close to the street that the greater part of the original lawn with its fine old trees lay behind it. There were once crape myrtle and syringa and lilac and jasmine bushes without order, and massed honeysuckle on fences and tree trunks; and after the first house had burned, these had taken the place and made of its shaggy informality a mazed and scented jungle loved of mocking-birds and thrushes, where boys and girls lingered on spring and summer nights among drifting fireflies and choiring whip-poor-wills and usually the liquid tremolo of a screech owl. Then the hill-man had bought it and cut some of the trees in order to build his house near the street after the country fashion.... (pp. 24–26)

To build a house close to the street is "after the country fashion" because the Mississippi hill farmer often built his farmhouse close to the road to enjoy the proximity of commerce. The next step for these aspiring hill-folk was usually to move into town and make a go of it. The beginning of the movement from farm to city that began after World War I is seen here in the "street of lesser residences, mostly new" (p. 165), which Horace and Narcissa drive through on their way home: "tight little houses with a minimum of lawn, homes built by country-bred people and set close to the street after the country fashion" (pp. 165-66). Their destination, the Benbow house, is in another area of town, where "the street opened away between old shady lawns, spacious and quiet. These homes were quite old, in appearance at least, and set well back from the street and its dust, they emanated a gracious and benign peace..." (pp. 168-69). In being "set well back from the street," the Benbow house is associated with the older town homes of Jefferson, homes generating a lyric peacefulness in the flower gardens made possible by their large front lawns.

Both of these pieces of landscape once held such gardens. The Mitchells' was once the "mazed and scented jungle" of the passage above and this lyric garden is a more intense version of the Benbow's terraced lawn, where young girls pick the scattered flowers of the once formal bed and "neighbors' children [play] among them and beneath the cedars" (p. 170). The succession of landscaping from Francis Benbow's terraced lawn with formal garden to Will's careless destruction of it and its stubborn reblooming suggests a gradual disordering of the lives of those who live there. But the implication of the fictive landscape is not rendered apparent in the circumstances of the Benbow's lives, a kind of flaw which might be expected in an early novel. The remarkable thing is that Faulkner's sense of architecture and landscape as meaningful is fully developed even in this first Yoknapatawpha novel, and only his application of it within the craft of fiction is as yet imperfect.

The significance of an individual thing or element is much more under the author's control. Narcissa, for instance, is constantly associated with and analogized to crystal. Perhaps both she and Horace are of that same fragile and delicate nature, since not only is his hobby glass-blowing (p. 171), but the words he speaks to himself at one point concerning his return to his life at home with his sister ("the meaning of peace") "linger with a dying fall pure as silver and crystal struck lightly together" (p. 176). If Horace is the silver in this simile, it is substantiated only by his naming his second vase after his sister (p. 182). The analogy is continued by Miss Jenny's remark on Bayard and Narcissa's "seeming obliviousness of one another. 'He treats her like a dog would treat a cut-glass pitcher, and she looks at him like a cut-glass pitcher would look at a dog,'..." (p. 205). Long after Bayard and Narcissa are married, Narcy returns to her house to visit Horace, and in her room she notices that the dressing table "was bare of its intimate silver and crystal" (p. 300).

Narcissa's brief return to her room speaks much of her sense of dwelling in it and within time. After finding the withered flowers (a rather obvious and perhaps overdone symbol of her now consumated state) and throwing them out the window, she finds the room "too chill to stop in long, and she decided to ask Eunice to build a fire on the hearth for the comfort of that part of her which still lingered here" (p. 300). Though physical warmth is the implication, it is a psychic part of Narcissa which still dwells in her bedroom, and that part requires the psychic comfort of a fire on its hearth, the sign of a living presence. It is this warmth she seeks when she quits the room for the living room downstairs, which has a fire going on its hearth.

Narcissa dwells among the things of the Benbow house. Special to her are her dressing table and chest of drawers, the hearth and the piano. The now empty dressing table no longer holds much attention, but the chest of drawers is very much one of Gaston Bachelard's "hiding-places in which human beings . . . keep or hide their secrets."[10] Narcissa has a very intimate involvement with the drawers which held the anonymous letters, and they allow her to enter again "into the closed circle of her bewilderment" (p. 300). But they provide no consolation for her anxiety, nor does the bedroom hearth for the chill of her spirit. Still she lingers in this private space to consider her most private secret, and only quits the room when she reawakens from her daydream to recall that this "should be Horace's day" as well as her own. That is, she recalls that this time, this day, is to take place in another room, a less private one, and one which may offer some psychic warmth. She finds her way to the fire in the living room and then seeks out the other object where a part of her still lingers: her piano.

In dwellings which have a piano, this instrument becomes another traditional focus besides fireplace, bed, and dining table. As both musical instrument and piece of furniture, the piano gathers others around as a fireplace or dining table does. Yet even in the largest of such gatherings, the player enters into a very personal relationship with it, as intimate as any with a chest of drawers or wardrobe. The player gives of himself to the piano through the craft of his playing and the piano renders forth in music a response which is an expression from the player's soul. The piano is the voice of its player's soul.[11]

Narcissa seeks out the piano when she is searching for peace. While visiting Miss Jenny at Sartoris, she is distressed by the vision of Bayard standing in the parlor door and shrinks against the Sartoris piano. After seeing him on the wild stallion in town she is again distraught and tries to play both before and after she calls Miss Jenny to inquire about Bayard's condition. She cries as she plays before telling Miss Jenny of her concern for Horace's consorting with Belle Mitchell, and she cries on the closed lid of the piano while she waits to resume reading to the bedridden Bayard.

On the day she returns to her house to spend the day with Horace, she retreats from her bedroom to find a fire on the living room hearth. But her piano has not been moved from the alcove to the living room, as is customary by this time of year. So, forced to choose between hearth and piano, she returns to the warmth of the living room.

There is in *Sartoris* the outline of a vertical relationship of man to the plane of the landscape, a bipolar relationship of man between earth and sky. The participants are young John and Bayard. Though young Bayard is quite wild in an automobile, he is relatively calm while standing on the earth and working with it: "For a time the earth held him in a hiatus that might have been called contentment. He was up at sunrise, planting things in the ground and watching them grow and tending them" (p. 203). Since he has no biplane, Bayard inhabits the sky only in dreams, or fresh from them: "Then, momentarily, the world was laid away and he was a trapped beast in the high blue, mad for life, trapped in the very cunning fabric that had betrayed him who had dared chance too much..." (p. 203). It is unclear whether the reference here is to Bayard's brother or to Daedalus, but the point is clear: the farther one is from earth, the more daring, Daedalian, abstract, and Apollonian he becomes. Neither young Bayard nor his brother has achieved the wisdom not to lose the dream in the seeking of it. In reaching too high, young John loses his life, and his epitaph, "I bare him on eagles' wings/and brought him unto Me," is almost literally true; Bayard saw him fall from his plane into a cloud but never saw him fall out again to earth.

After John is killed, Bayard continues to seek whatever it is his brother was pursuing. Just exactly what this is never clearly articulated by Faulkner, unless it is implied by the "Time and its furniture" metaphor as the wisdom not to lose the dream in the seeking of it. The idea that Time might teach him such wisdom is rejected by Bayard in rejecting Time's furniture, the meaningful remnants in his brother's closet chest. The standard critical assessment of Bayard is to dismiss him as another rootless modern, given too much to abstraction and the unreal. But he has no truly abstract tendencies as, for instance, do Cervantes's Quixote or Dostoevsky's Prince Mishkin. The error is to seek the dream too vaguely, thereby losing it. The right way, learned from Time and its furniture, is to concretize the dream, to bring it into the real, the definite, the concrete. Colonel Sartoris embodied his dream in his house and affirmed it by rebuilding it after the war. Young Bayard's vacuum is a lack of dreams of the right kind; he has no dreams of aspiration, only dreams of past events he cannot escape. Confused, he loses the dream he ought to seek and instead seeks to concretize his dream of young John's death by making it into the real event of his own death.

The true opposite of concretizing the dream, however, is to attempt the concretization of something less than a dream, a private notion or the private self. Sartoris builds a home which, in being lived in by a patriarch, becomes an image of a way of life, an icon for the commmunity. Thomas Sutpen consciously designs a house to be an image of himself and an icon of his family, a mask of respectability and nothing more. *Absalom, Absalom!,* Faulkner's other novel concerned with a particular manor house, relates not the "setting-into-work" of truth or the truth of the dream, but rather the setting into work of a lie. As Sartoris and Sutpen are opposites in person, so Sartoris the place and Sutpen's Hundred are two pieces of antithetical fictive architecture.

4

Absalom, Absalom!:
"Something Like a Wing of Versailles"

Absalom, Absalom! takes place, literally, in but half a dozen rooms in two or three structures, within a small community and part of its purlieu. Whereas the Sartoris house is a kind of stage setting for the action of *The Unvanquished* and *Sartoris/Flags in the Dust*, and the De Spain house in "Barn Burning" is a directly influential symbolic object, Sutpen's mansion is, more than other elements of Yoknapatawpha, an extension and manifestation of this man and a representation of what happens to his family and to the "idea" Sutpen.

The two estates of Sartoris and Sutpen's Hundred make an interesting contrast. Sartoris itself is named, of course, for the family, and the name, in its own way, is an attribute or quality. Sutpen's Hundred is named for the number of square miles it contains—a quantity. The complete name is composed of two words: the possessive form of the owner's name and the quantitative measurement of what is possessed. Sophonsiba Beauchamp's repeated reference to Hubert's place as "Warwick" presents the opposite extreme of the practice of naming a place, for hers is a more imaginative, more poetic, and certainly one of the more romantic names for a Yoknapatawpha manor. In any case, the naming of the place indicates the attitude of the dweller, and in Sutpen's case reveals his penchant for applying accountancy to matters of human amenity and values.

Nothing of this tendency has escaped Sutpen's neighbors, and their epithetical descriptions of other manor houses are also noteworthy. The cumulative significance of Drusilla's definitive remark on Sartoris as "the aura of father's dream" recalls the comparable phrase for McCaslin which occurs in "The Bear," where Carothers's unfinished mansion is described as "the concrete indication of his own vanity's boundless conceiving" (GDM, p. 262). The most illustrative of such epithets uttered concerning the Sutpen house, however, is not from *Absalom, Absalom!* but from *Requiem for a Nun*, where the house is described as "something like a wing of Versailles glimpsed in a Lilliput's gothic nightmare" (RFN, p. 40). These words are more than a pithy stylistic rendering of the house and its outbuildings. The word "gothic" here, in lower case, applies the gothic aura to the metaphorical Lilliputian's nightmare only, not to the house. The allusion to Versailles, however, suggests the presence of French Baroque details in the stylistic vocabulary of the house, provides a reference for conjecturing overall dimensions, and recommends certain images of grandeur and scale. Compared to Drusilla's words on Sartoris, it balances the architectural image in a small scale nightmare with the aura of an architectural symbol in an heroic dream.

Further elaboration of this epithet arises from Christian Norberg-Schulz's description of the Baroque garden-palace:

> a horizontally extended geometrical network of paths which concretizes the absolutist pretentions of the Sovereign located at the centre of the system. The centre is moreover used to divide the "world" in two halves: a man-made, urban environment on one side, and "infinitely" extended nature on the other. Close to the centre nature appears as a cultural landscape (*parterre*), further away it becomes more "natural" (*bosquet*), to end in a "wilderness." [1]

Much of this description is directly applicable to Sutpen's Hundred and the sovereign located at its center. Certain it is that Sutpen has absolutist pretentions, albeit on a Lilliputian scale. Frequent allusions to the fact that the entire place rises almost *ex nihilo* from the alluvial swamp generate the visionary site plan of a man-made structure set at the center of a vast tract of wilderness. Norberg-Schulz's concluding remarks on the garden-palace refer to the "classical derivation" of the palace as well as the cosmic implications of its strict axial and symmetrical grandeur. Sutpen's strident effort in forging his mark on the earth admits of a Promethean will of irresistable pretentions, reflected also in the theocratic air Rosa attributes to him in the command "*Be Sutpen's Hundred.*"

There are few other passages in *Absalom* or other novels to aid visualization of Sutpen's house or plantation. What the place "looks like" and what it means must be distilled from a catalog of particulars drawn from the novel and from two other probable influences. It is no error to assume that Pettibone's Tidewater plantation and the elder Bon's Haitian one were of sufficient influence to make Sutpen's somewhat grander than the conventional four-columned porticoes of the local building tradition. Further, the hand and eye of the French architect must not be dismissed, especially if his own will is as strong as indicated in the design of Jefferson's courthouse and square in *Requiem*.

A catalog appraisal of the Sutpen place includes a number of interesting aspects. The "Hundred" of Sutpen's Hundred is one hundred square miles (or sections) "of some of the best virgin bottom land in the country" (p. 34). Miss Rosa's remark to Quentin is that the plantation is called Sutpen's Hundred "as if it had been a king's grant in unbroken perpetuity from his great grandfather—a home" (p. 16). There is no reason to doubt Rosa's point here. Part of Sutpen's design is precisely the image of perpetuity—permanence, long-standing, enduring heritage, a local habitation and a name etched against contingency.

The plantation contains formal gardens and flower beds (which have no flowers until Sutpen marries Ellen three years after completing the house and which are "ruined and weed choked" in 1862), promenades, slave quarters, stables, pastures, smokehouses, a scuppernong arbor, and an entrance gate half a mile from the manor house, inside of which is a park, with a grove of cedar and oak trees surrounding the home itself. There is a fishing camp on the south bank of the Tallahatchie River and, after the war, a crossroads store on the land.

Whether Sutpen's acreage could fit in the quadrant of Yoknapatawpha where Faulkner locates it might present a problem, but the solution is that it does not have to. The fact that the house itself is "set in the middle of the domain" (p. 213) requires that there be but five miles between the house and any cardinal boundary. The road to Jefferson is a southeast/northwest diagonal which, if the tract is roughly square, would permit Sutpen (or anyone) to ride a little over seven miles to arrive at the corner of his land. Early in the novel Sutpen is said to live "eight miles from any neighbor" (p. 39), and since the map and the other novels place Sartoris four miles from Jefferson, he is most probably Sutpen's only neighbor. Quentin's remark that Sutpen "at one time could have galloped for ten miles in any direction without crossing his own boundary" (p. 182), though not an exaggeration, is valid only if the rider began at one boundary and rode in the opposite cardinal direction (e.g., from the western boundary due east). The same dimensions require that Sutpen's land lie partially across the Tallahatchie, since the hunting and fishing camp where Wash Jones lives is nearly at the bank of the river and only about three miles from the run-down slave quarters where he fetches the old Negress who is midwife for his granddaughter (p. 286).

The fishing camp is a study unto itself. Built sometime after 1838, "after the first woman—Ellen—entered the house and the last deer and bear hunter went out of it" (p. 125), it is already "abandoned and rotting" by 1860 when Jones, his daughter, and granddaughter are living there. Though in *Go Down, Moses*, Major de Spain has bought and restored the camp in 1865 when the hunting parties begin, in *Absalom* it still belongs to Sutpen and is the scene of his murder by Wash.

Though both camps are geographically one and the same, the fishing camp of *Absalom* is a profoundly different *place*. It is not part of the wilderness of *Go Down, Moses;* it is something topologically other. The character of the entire region, the plantation, the swamp and the fishing camp, is that of a *purlieu.* Jason Compson's offhand use of the word in a simile for Sutpen's Hundred—"a shadowy miasmic region something like the bitter purlieus of Styx" (p. 69)—disguises the accuracy and appropriateness of the term. The entire area is a lawless hinterland under Sutpen's sole control, where men no longer hunt animals but other men. The fishing camp, site of a triple homicide and suicide, becomes the darkest part of this purlieu and quite another place than that where Isaac McCaslin feels the presence of the sentient immortal Umpire.

Another of Jason Compson's similes suggests that Bon finds Sutpen's Hundred to be "a brawling and childish and quite deadly mud-castle household in a miasmic and spirit-ridden forest" (p. 93). And though the house itself does possess a sentient spirit apart from the beings who dwell in it, the details of the mansion ought to be examined first.

Sutpen erects his house, nearly *ex nihilo,* out of the very swamp itself. The townspeople, it is said, "watch his mansion rise, carried plank by plank and brick by brick out of the swamp where the clay and timber waited" (p. 37). Forged out of the earth itself, rising directly out of the elements, it is probably composed of cypress and alluvial clay and stands within a grove of cedar and oak (p. 38). The building of a brick kiln on-site is not unusual in such early house construction, and it is noted later in *Requiem for a Nun* that Sutpen's architect designs and builds another kiln to make the bricks for Jefferson's courthouse. However in the present novel not only is the courthouse already built, but it is used as a referent for the dimensions of Sutpen's house, which are not specifically determinable from the text. It is Miss Rosa who first mentions that it is "the size of a court house" (p. 16), while Jason Compson's more verbose remarks describe it as "the half-acre gunroom of a baronial splendor... the Spartan shell of the largest edifice in the county, not excepting the courthouse itself" (p. 39).[2]

Something of the character of the place can be derived from the frequent use of fortification terminology. "Gunroom" is, of course, strictly military. But Rosa has already suggested that her sister, after marrying Sutpen, "had vanished into the stronghold of an ogre" (p. 23) or, as Compson says, "an edifice like Bluebeard's" (p. 60). Most significant, however, is Quentin's father's lengthy remark on the need for Sutpen's architect to scale down the originally intended design; "the dream of grim and castlelike magnificence at which Sutpen obviously aimed" (p. 38). "Castlelike" here is probably more of an impressionistic than a stylistic criticism, and ties in with the other references to Bluebeard and his castle.

In the matter of scale, "the place as Sutpen planned it," Faulkner says, "would have been almost as large as Jefferson itself at the time" (p. 38). The reader has been told, only six pages before, just exactly how large Jefferson is at the time: "a village then: the Holston House, the courthouse, six stores, a blacksmith and livery stable, a saloon frequented by drovers and peddlers, three churches and perhaps thirty residences..." (p. 32). The paragraph following Compson's remark on Sutpen's original design is the well-known catalog of the entire immediate architectural site of Sutpen's place, "its formal gardens and promenades, its slave quarters and stables and smokehouses" (p. 39). Juxtaposition of these two descriptions shows that Sutpen's original architectural intention was for a mansion as large as Holston House and the courthouse combined. The French architect curbed this intention to a house "the size of a courthouse." The remaining correspondences can be seen in a comparison of the two catalogs:

Holston House courthouse	—mansion
six stores	—smokehouses
blacksmith livery	—stables
saloon	—promenades
three churches	—formal gardens
thirty residences	—slave quarters

Little can be said of the site plan of Sutpen's mansion and its outbuildings. Gunroom metaphors and castle images aside, placement of the structures is only suggested by references such as the one which notes that the men who come to watch Sutpen and his negroes fight tie their horses "in the grove beyond the stable and so come up across the pasture unseen from the house" (p. 28). Grove and house are on a hill (p. 29), and the road up to the house from the gate is a half-mile long. To conjecture a plan at all one needs to begin with a central hall, in which Thomas sets up his gravestone after placing Ellen's on her grave. The hall then becomes a room of cessation and stasis instead of an axis of activity and movement. If the kitchen is assumed to be in its customary right rear corner of the first floor, it is the upstairs bedroom in the right rear where Bon lies as Wash Jones builds his coffin out of boards from the carriage house (and another node of activity becomes an enclosure for death), in the back yard "right under the back parlor [left rear] window" (p. 151). Though Judith, Rosa, and Clytie all sleep in the same room while waiting for Thomas to return from the War, which room it is cannot be known. There is, however, Rosa's curious remark which, like those concerning the fishing camps of *Absalom* and "The Bear," distinguishes two places extant in one space, separated only by time: "We kept the room which Thomas Sutpen would return to—not that one which he left, a husband, but the one to which he should return a sonless widower" (p. 155). Faulkner's fiction seems to contain many statements like this which indicate that the station and circumstance of the inhabitant define the nature of the space he inhabits. A change in condition or stature brings an accompanying change in the space of the enclosure in which he dwells. This change occurs whether or not he has returned, and whether or not he brings with him the artifacts and objects which speak, however mutely, of that condition or circumstance.

It remains a paradox for Thomas Sutpen that, though his eye is focused on the edifice he builds and his brain on what he desires it to express, it is these details at the basic level of architectural symbol which reveal so much about him. Early on, in 1835, when the house stands "without a window or door or bedstead in it" (p. 16), "without a pane of glass or a doorknob or hinge" (p. 39), Sutpen has already been indicted by the community precisely for the absence of these details, the things for which he feels he has no need.

It is not difficult to grasp the sense of the community's complaint. The objects close to our hands and our senses are the the objects through which we participate in existence. They are the media by which we enjoy the amenities, the intangible. Were we all strictly functional beings, we would all live under simple pavilions, the literal "roof over our heads." Put another way, it is not because we are civilized that the cave fire has become the fireplace and hearth; it is because we have the need to make the object become artifact, to transform necessity into custom, ritual, tradition, meaning. Norberg-Schulz mentions the hearth, the dining table, and the bed as the three points of focus in the house, and these are exactly the things Sutpen's house does not have. Without windows, window glass and doors, his dwelling has no inside/outside relationship. There is no dining table, and no hearth is mentioned, though there must be at least four. There is no bed, only a pallet. Without these, there are no human relationships inside the dwelling. Though a strictly practical man would say Sutpen lives without that which he has no need of, it is closer to the truth to say that he exhibits what the philosopher Frederick Wilhelmsen calls ontological poverty.[3] He has no sense of the meaningful and cares nothing for that which he needs to live fully; he possesses things not to enjoy them but only to have acquired them.

The things of existence in the Sutpen mansion are eventually acquired, of course, but only because Sutpen knows he needs them to gain a wife; or, as Compson has it, "not the least of which furniture was that wedding license" (p. 51). Eventually everything, all the trappings of his design, is in place: "the windows and doors and the spits and pots in the kitchen and the crystal chandeliers in the parlors and the [mahogany] furniture and the curtains and the rugs" (p. 44). There is a dining table (p. 64), and the door is there too, though it is mentioned only much later: a "formal door beneath its fanlight imported pane by pane from Europe" (p. 184). The window and door exist one upon the other.

It is curious that the door is mentioned only long after the life of the house has begun its decline. Of greater interest is the isolated nature of the life of the house, which is never seen as a whole, complete, vital dwelling interacting with its inhabitants. The mansions of both the English manor house and plantation novel traditions, Sartoris included, are functionally symbolic pieces of fictive architecture whose meanings are extrusions of the life lived within them, the life and the meaning interconnected. But the pattern of *Absalom* presents the reader with a vision of a slowly decaying house while the story is told in his ear. Except for the last conflagration scene, this action of the life of the house is something separate from the life of the Sutpens; the house is related to its family in the mode of a simile rather than a metaphor. The house is seen in detailed study only when it is either "the Spartan shell of the largest edifice" (p. 39) before Ellen comes, or "a shell marooned and forgotten in the backwater of catastrophe—a skeleton" (p. 132) after the war, or as a rotting house ever afterward. Twenty years of what might be called its normal life are not depicted, are not a part of the representative history of the house.

Again from the point of view of other fictive architecture, little if any of the action of *Absalom, Absalom!* takes place within the house. Except for Sutpen's meeting with Henry in the library and Quentin's creeping through the parlor to get to the front door when Rosa and he try to break into the house, no one is depicted in the first floor rooms. Rosa's reflections on eating in the kitchen below the room where Bon's body lies and on existence with Judith while waiting for Sutpen to return home are general recollections, and only her remark about keeping Sutpen's room clean is expressive of meaningful space. The only other major actions are Clytie's restraint of Rosa from the hall stairs as Bon and, later, Henry die in the bedroom above. Put more succinctly, the only events in the Sutpen house are Henry's warning in the library, Clytie's restraint in the hall, and the three (or, actually, five) deaths upstairs.

There are no acts of love in the house. The only action in the library is ultimatum, denial, and repudiation. In the hall there is only challenge, restraint, and defiance. In the bedroom upstairs there is only sickness (Judith's) and death.

The house, however, has the capacity to remember, and its strongest attribute throughout the novel is its sentient quality, its knowing perception and memory. Both Jason Compson and Rosa allude to this attribute of the house. Compson tries to express the static oblivion into which Judith and Charles seem to fall when Ellen speaks of them: "Their joys and griefs must now be forgotten even by the very boards on which they had strutted and postured and laughed and wept" (p. 75); and Rosa, who queries herself as to whom she expected to find in the upstairs hall when she came to Sutpen's Hundred responding to the news of Bon's death (at the hand of Henry), answers, "Henry perhaps, to emerge from some door which knew his touch, his hand on the knob, the weight of his foot on a sill which knew that weight" (pp. 140–41).

The first of these two remarks attributes to the house an awareness of the past, the accumulated history of a family recorded on its everyday flooring, which past must now be forgotten. The second remark attributes to the house a knowledge of *person* (Henry) by his tread and by his physical interaction with some of its elements.[4]

So the house knows its past, and it knows its people. Yet to Rosa and to the reader, the most remarkable part of its nature is not its quality of memory but what Rosa calls "the living spirit, presence, of that house" (p. 27), not the structure's awareness of others, but its own perceptible consciousness. Jason Compson is most descriptive of this spirit, despite the fact that his use of conjunctive simile indicates he does not believe it: "as though houses actually possess a sentience, a personality and character acquired not so much from the people who breathe or have breathed in them inherent in the wood or brick or begotten upon the wood or brick by the man or men who conceived and built them ... " (p. 85).

Jason Compson suggests here that the house seems to have a personality that is determined to deny its existential purpose. He describes it clearly as "an incontrovertible affirmation for emptiness, desertion; an insurmountable resistance to occupancy save when sanctioned and protected by the ruthless and the strong" (p. 85). Since to dwell is to live in a meaningful place,[5] the two-fold purpose of a house is to contain life and be meaningful. The question is thus: "How can a house, especially one which seems to possess character and person, deny its very purpose?" The answer can be found in the building intention.

The purpose of building a house is to create a meaningful place to dwell. But whatever Sutpen "gets" on the earth—slaves, land, furniture, wedding license, wife or children—he acquires only for the purpose of appropriation; only to be having it. When the house is created ("*Be Sutpen's Hundred*") with this intention, it is not a dwelling but a possessed object wanted and had, but not loved.

It is possible to speak here of two kinds of building/dwelling as Wilhelmsen writes of two kinds of love, *eros* and *agape*.[6] One can build or dwell merely to seek one's own perfection, as all things do (*eros*), or to affirm the "richness of his existence" by experiencing the place as meaningful (dwelling in *agape*). Sutpen dwells inauthentically, because he seeks his own perfection not by living a meaningful existence, but by appropriating the house to his own being, as the inauthentic lover appropriates that which he loves to himself, "to overcome his own ontological poverty."

Further, the house is not "let be," as Heidegger says, by allowing it to come into that perfection which is the hope and destiny of all houses. The mansion is not built to be a dwelling but to be a possession, not a place but an appropriated object. Existence within it is not permitted to become meaning, nor is the house permitted to give of itself to man. Hence it resists dwelling, and only permits occupancy "when sanctioned by the ruthless and the strong" (p. 85).

But a single character's denial of meaningful intention to a piece of fictive architecture inhibits neither its sentience nor its ability to be meaningful for either character and reader. It continues to manifest sentience and personality, and although it goes on to become more of an icon of the family's history, during the interim of the war and Henry's murder of Charles Bon it betrays, to Rosa again, the darkness of despair. Calling for Judith in the lower hall, Rosa hears the echo, not of her own voice, but of the ghost which now haunts Sutpen's Hundred in the person of its lost hopes:[7]

> an echo spoke which was not mine but rather that of the lost irrevocable might-have-been which haunts all houses, all enclosed walls erected by human hands, not for shelter, not for warmth, but to hide from the world's curious looking and seeing the dark turnings which the ancient young delusions of pride and hope and ambition . . . take. (p. 137)

Here, then, is the curious occurrence of emotions—the fear, grief, joy, longing, hope, and despair which are generated by meaningful dwelling— becoming themselves the spirits which haunt the house whose person knows intimately the people and events that generated those emotions.

When at length the house does assume the full iconic stature of imaging the idea Sutpen, it is a gradual fulfillment of Rosa's supposition as to why the house survives the war:

> Rotting portico and scaling walls, it stood, not ravaged, not invaded, marked by no bullet nor soldier's iron heel but rather as though reserved for something more: some desolation more profound than ruin, as if it had stood in iron juxtaposition to flame, to a holocaust which had found itself less fierce and less implacable, not hurled but rather fallen back before the impervious and indomitable skeleton which the flames durst not, at the instant's final crisis, assail. . . . (p. 136)[8]

Knowingly or not, Rosa foretells the catastrophic end of the mansion, which survives the fire of war only to collapse in a "desolation more profound than ruin," an inferno which consumes its last inhabitants. The "skeleton" is the frame to the "body" of the house, whose consciousness is "the waiting grim decaying presence, spirit, of the house itself" (p. 160), to whom Sutpen seems to be talking in the evenings after he returns. The entirety of the plantation is so much a part of him that he can speak to it. He has appropriated all of it to his own being, to the extent that he has become its possession, and its physical deterioration reveals Sutpen's own moral dissolution, "a part of him encompassing each ruined field and fallen fence and crumbling wall of cabin or cotton house or crib" (p. 160). The curious point about Rosa's thought here is that, although there are certainly parts of the plantation which are in fair shape after only four years of neglect, Sutpen's being is affiliated exclusively with the decaying parts of his domain. It is only those ruined, fallen, and crumbling parts of the site which Sutpen inhabits.

5

Jefferson:
The Urban Design of a Fictive Small Town

The fictive plantation manor presents an image of a home as the center of a domain and characterizes the nature of the family that dwells there. Fictive townhouses generally may have as much to say about the families who inhabit them, though the associations have more to do with communal interaction. The purpose of town life, after all, is the commonweal, communal order; and all townhouse life is in some way directed toward this center.

The center of Jefferson is the embodiment of its communal order in a simple form, the Yoknapatawpha County Courthouse. It is the single most important piece of fictive architecture in Faulkner's work. However, its significance in *Requiem for a Nun* cannot be articulated separately from the significance of Jefferson, since it embodies the *raison d'être* for the town itself. The explication of the Yoknapatawpha County Courthouse, then, is not that of a single structure, but that of one built form as a center for a gathering of other built forms, the interrelationship of which fulfills the design intention of making a town, the practice of community. Accordingly, it is important to detail the architectural content of the town of Jefferson first, and then examine its founding through the establishment of law and its embodiment in the courthouse.

The town of Jefferson is fictive architecture at the urban level. As such it has both its own particular history, as seen in *Requiem for a Nun*, and a certain position in the development of urban form. The town center is both a public interior space and a form on the landscape. Historically (as will be discussed later) it is first a Chickasaw trading post, then a settlement, a village, a town, and a county seat.

Cartographically, Jefferson has an orthogonal and biaxially symmetrical town square geometrically aligned with the cardinal points, with the north-south orientation predominant.[1] The street pattern is a tight grid close in to the north-south and east-west axes but unravels as it extends out in each quadrant, where the pattern becomes more topologically articulated. Only the north and south approaches to the town offer a front facade view of the courthouse and may be considered the principal entry, vista, and main axis of circulation. This schema, together with the fact that the balance of the town lies to the north, depicts south-to-north continuity by drawing circulation along this principal axis.

Much of the significance of the town plan of Jefferson is to be derived from its place in the historical development of the urban design process, and its rigid geometrical plan is the determinant factor. Though there are exceptions,[2] Classical Greek poleis such as Athens, Delphi, Delos, and Olympia, were topologically organized arrangements of individual geometrical forms, making use of the values of proximity and enclosure rather than axiality. These balanced arrangements of architectural forms on the landscape, among which the Classical Athenian agora is the best-known example, were empirical responses to natural topography and the patterns of everyday commerce and ritual. They were responses to a human sense of order within our own being which is not translatable in geometric or orthogonal form. By the middle of the fifth century B.C., however, Miletus, Priene, and even the Athenian port at the Piraeus were exhibiting, under the influence of Hippodamus and others, gridiron street plans and rectangular agoras. As these cities developed and others fell to be rebuilt in the Hellenistic and then Roman eras, the design of urban spaces became increasingly axial, symmetrical, and orthogonal, until in Roman times most major areas were square or rectangular in plan, and new settlements were based on the Roman *campus.*[3] The rigid geometry set into the landscape reflected an evermore measured and technological society. As Greek culture became Hellenistic acculturation and then Roman civilization, town design began more and more to superimpose the grid on the landscape.

The process of designing an axially symmetrical town square is thus a Roman act, and the insistently geometrical town planning of Sutpen's Parisian architect is an Hellenistic gesture for Habersham's community. It is an analog for the movement from compactness to differentiation suffered by all communities, a movement from a generally emotional and undisciplined collective settlement to a more disciplined political form reflected in the disciplined design of its figure/ground. The formation of Jefferson's square is thus a metaphor of the community's graduation from *themis* to *dike* in its political order, which takes place in the story of the Trace bandits, Holston's lock, and the founding of the town as a county seat.

But the plan of Sutpen's architect must still be considered a conscious design superimposed in a Roman way on a town which would otherwise have developed, organically and empirically, in a Greek way. Though it may be safe to assume the continued influence of Greek tendencies like spatial awareness

Figure 5-1. The Orthogonal Town Squares of Oxford and Jefferson

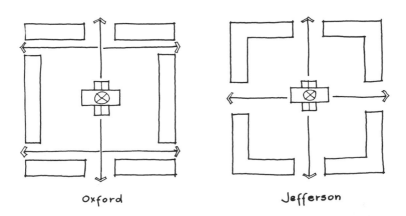

in the topological and organic responses of the nonorthogonal streets of both Oxford and Jefferson, the particular shape of the enclosure which the Parisian designs in the Jefferson square is distinctly Roman, even more so than the square in Oxford. A figure drawing of the mass elements of both shows Jefferson as an example of Jere French's observations about Roman space; that it is "closed or appears to be closed at all the corners, entrance usually occurring in the center of a side" and that "Roman space is static in the sense that symmetrical balance, rigid axiality, centric placement of elements, and monumentality of scale are emphasized."[4] Though most of these characteristics apply to both Oxford and its fictional descendant, it is Jefferson's biaxial design which closes the corners of its town square, horizontally frames its monumental courthouse, and arrests the enclosed space in which it stands.

The Parisian architect's design process puts him on the Roman side of the eighteenth-century French quarrel about Greek and Roman architecture,[5] but the form he creates in Jefferson is a derivative of the European urban design tradition. As a historic type, Jefferson's courthouse square is not only a familiar one in the American South, but a culminant paradigm composed of the best elements of European models. The reasons for its occurrence involve the forms which urban space had taken by the mid-nineteenth century, and the fact that westward expansion provided the opportunity of planning entire towns at a single stroke. Since medieval times urban space had taken the shape created by people gathering around some center at which they erected the symbol of their faith—temple, church, or cathedral. The transmigration to the New World, the political founding of a new country combined with large expanses of territory in which to lay out whole towns on the grid pattern produced, especially in the period of 1820–1900, the rise of the courthouse town. The real significance of this form is best expressed by Collin Rowe:

> For these courthouse squares are not the residential enclosures of England, nor like the piazzas of Italy do they admit the church in a presiding role. Here it is law which assumes a public significance; it is around the secular image of law, like architectural illustrations of a political principle, that these towns revolve. In each case the courthouse is both focus and social guarantee; and in each square the reality of government made formally explicit provides the continuing assurance of order.[6]

Historically, this type of town square form derives from a body of design instructions called the Laws of the Indies, a prescriptive code extant since the sixteenth century in the Spanish and French West Indies. Published in 1573, it was used extensively and almost exclusively in the design of Spanish towns in the New World. Though Sutpen's architect is called Parisian, Sutpen captures him as he practices in Haiti. This Carribean setting is, of course, his origin and the place of his training and education. Given the historical moment and environment, the Laws seem an obvious source for the architect's design of Jefferson. At one point, Faulkner's description of the event and the architect's words seem a very close paraphrase of one paragraph in the ordinances: "The plan of the place, with its squares, streets and building lots is to be outlined by means of measuring by cord and ruler, beginning with the main square from which streets are to run to the gates and principal roads and leaving sufficient open space so that even if the town grows it can always spread in a symmetrical manner."[7] The Laws prescribe the dimensions and orientation of open town squares, with public buildings fronting the open central forum. These squares, however, have no central public building. Much consideration must be given the transmission of these designs to both the south and east coasts and the early occurrences of the central formal courthouse, with lawns and gardens, in the county seats of Tidewater, Virginia, as well as their migration westward to form six basic types of courthouse square. The archetype of these is called the "Shelbyville" square, after that in Shelbyville, Tennessee, from which developed the "Harrisonburg" type, of which Oxford is representative, and the "Lancaster" square with biaxial streets, which distinguishes Jefferson from Oxford. (See fig. 5–2.)[8]

The form of the courthouse town intensified as it spread, and most of its finest examples are in Mississippi and Texas. In terms of the progressive development of this form, Jefferson's town square is even better than Oxford's, because the fictive square is closer to the paradigm of its European ancestors.

As urban form, the public spaces of Europe usually consist of an open irregular enclosure (Piazza del Cisterna), often centered with a monument or

Figure 5-2. Types of Courthouse Squares

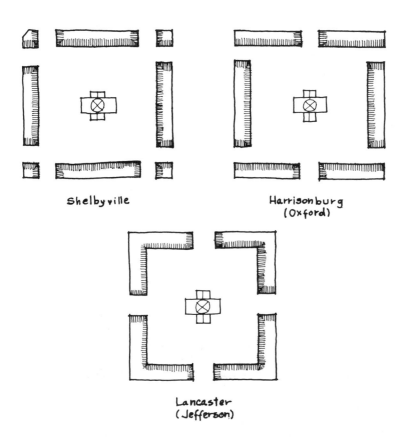

Shelbyville

Harrisonburg
(Oxford)

Lancaster
(Jefferson)

fountain, sometimes surrounding or enclosing a public building or church. Occasionally the space forms a forecourt to a public or sacred building at one end (Todi), or the enclosure is simply a small park or green space. The town squares of the American South in general and of Oxford and Jefferson in particular are a composite of the best of these forms in a secular New World. They represent the collective paradigm of the public building as sacred monument in a park. Faulkner's concise description in *Requiem for a Nun* is a catalog of its elements: "a Square, the courthouse in its grove the center; quadrangular around it, the stores, two-storey, the offices of the lawyers and doctors and dentists, the lodge-rooms and auditoriums, above them; school and church and tavern and bank and jail each in its ordered place, the four broad diverging avenues straight as plumb-lines in the four directions..." (p. 39).

Though the square is most noticeably an open space, an enclosure, Faulkner's description does not begin with this idea but with "the courthouse in its grove" as the center—not the building alone but the courthouse together with its surrounding greenspace as the central element. The town square is primarily (and most significantly) instituted law established on the land. The Parisian recognizes that Jefferson's courthouse is the "repository and guardian of the aspirations and the hopes" of its builders, and his placement of the courthouse reflects the sacrosanct respect the settlers hold for the law. The fact too that *dike* dwells in a park reflects the Southern piety for the Natural Law, its affinity with human law, and its necessary connection to leisure witnessed to in the amenity of a park.

Only secondarily is the square an enclosure; and the elements which form the enclosure are, importantly, offices of those in professions, with public gathering places above them. Though banks, drugstores and shops are more prominent in the squares of both Oxford and Jefferson, mercantile establishments are not mentioned in this catalog until all other public and professional uses have been listed. School and church are public gathering places, and tavern is mentioned before bank because the former is at once a gathering place and a business. The nineteenth-century drug and hardware stores might have been included here and, especially in Jefferson, the livery. The jail, on the other hand, is the antithesis of public gathering,[9] except, perhaps, in the chaotic mob scene of *Intruder in the Dust*.

This hierarchy of importance is maintained through the rest of the historical account. When the fire of war comes, the stores and shops are mentioned first—"two nights later, it was on fire (the Square, the stores and shops and the professional offices)" (p. 232)—after which it is postbellum economics that keeps them at the head of the list: "by New Year's of '66, the gutted walls... of the Square had been temporarily roofed and were stores and shops and offices again" (p. 237). Later still, as Jefferson roars into 1900, its visiting drummers are mentioned before the lawyers and court witnesses (p. 241).

Concurrent with this hierarchy is a natural one of tree and shade, the passing of which mirrors its own dissolution: "gone now were the last of the forest trees which had followed the shape of the Square, shading the unbroken second-storey balcony onto which the lawyers' and doctors' offices had opened, which shaded in its turn the fronts of the stores..." (p. 243).

The "four broad diverging avenues" are the elements which delineate the symmetry and enclosure of Jefferson and distinguish the fictive square most clearly from its factual counterpart. The specific axiality, however (not of the space as created by the space as created by process, but of the town square as a form) has additional effects. Because of the central place of the courthouse, axiality is both centripetal and centrifugal; vision and circulation both are drawn toward the square and look back down the vistas of the four avenues. The figure created by this centripetal collision of quadrangular axes recalls the Roman "Castra," a town form of which Timgad is the archetype.[10] Here the major elements are a north-south *cardo maximus* terminating at a center and an east-west main street, the *decumanus maximus.* In Jefferson, however, the north-south *cardo maximus* terminates at a positive center, rather than a negative central space, and then continues south, becoming the main street of the town by virtue of its frontal views of the courthouse. Meanwhile Faulkner's insertion of a single east-west street (instead of the two in Oxford—Jackson and Van Buren) gives Jefferson a *decumanus maximus,* albeit on the secondary axis, since it offers a side view of the courthouse. Entry up these east or west avenues is never described. Most of the planters live north or south of the town (Sartoris, Sutpen, Compson, Grenier), while the farmers and yeomen enter the town on the east-west axis (Lena Grove, the Armstids, and the Bundrens).[11]

As avenues of exit from the square, the four streets make the central space radial in its circulation pattern. But as a centric space, Jefferson's square is axial. It can also be said to be radial, since visual and directional thrust (towards the courthouse and outward from it) is in other directions than through the four vistas of its axial streets. Since both vision and circulation in a town square such as this can be directed to any of the offices or shops around its perimeter, any tension at an angle to the four axial streets asserts that the central space is radial as well as axial and centripetal or centrifugal in its radiality, according to whether the tension is from the outer edge of the square towards the courthouse or vice versa.

Finally, the south half of Jefferson's square delineates a kind of visual parvis before the courthouse. The south axis is the main entrance; the Confederate monument centers the space; and the south facade of the sacred political monument is the terminus. This south half of the square functions as a parvis in the fiction, particularly in *Requiem;* and the high point of its history is the mustering and swearing-in of the Jefferson regiment "which Sartoris as its colonel would take to Virginia" (p. 45). This event is mentioned twice in *Requiem,* the first time stating that Sartoris stands in the south balcony of the courthouse during the ceremony (at the center point of the terminus and the end point of the axis) and the second that the monument is indeed the exact center of this parvis: "the marble effigy—the stone infantryman on his stone pedestal on the exact spot where forty years ago the Richmond officer and the local Baptist minister had mustered in the Colonel's regiment . . ." (p. 239).

Jefferson's town square is a synthesis of the best elements of European

Figure 5-3.   Axial and Radial Elements in Jefferson

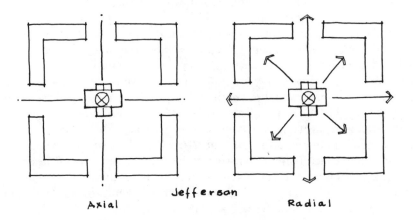

Axial   Jefferson   Radial

urban spaces. It is a close-knit enclosure on the scale of a residential square, centered by a building at once public, monumental and sacred, and set within a park. The square is both axial and radial, and its space is both centripetal and centrifugal. The events which take place in this fictive urban form constitute the story of the founding of Jefferson.

6

Requiem for a Nun:
"Symbol of the Aspirations and the Hopes"

In both the public and private orders of Yoknapatawpha, the meaning of architectural symbol is implied more often than it is stated. But the degree to which a construction of human hands can embody meaning and value is nowhere more explicit and intense in expression than in the rhapsodic account of the conception and planning of the Jefferson Courthouse in the Prologue to act 1 of *Requiem for a Nun*. On the literal level, the Prologue is simply the early history of Faulkner's county, but it is also the best example of the embodiment of the idea of community in a built form. It is the story of a community's self-acknowledgment as community and its realization of its own responsibilities.

The settlement which becomes Jefferson was organized

> by three men who were what was to be Yoknapatawpha County's coeval pioneers and settlers, leaving in it the three oldest names—Alexander Holston, who came as half groom and half bodyguard to Doctor Samuel Habersham, and half nurse and half tutor to the doctor's eight-year-old motherless son, the three of them riding horseback across Tennessee from the Cumberland Gap along with Louis Grenier, the Huguenot younger son who brought the first slaves into the country and was granted the first big land patent and so became the first cotton planter.... (p. 7)[1]

Holston brings with him from Carolina an enormous fifteen-pound lock "with a key almost as long as a bayonet" (p. 7). The lock is preeminently useless, since there is nothing in the settlement "behind the heavy bars and shutters needing further locking and securing" (p. 9). Yet the lock's size and very presence insist that it be used for something, and it is this demand which annoys the settlers. So the lock first comes to be used on the mail pouch delivered to the settlement about every two weeks. But even in this function it is useless, the pouch needing "a lock as little as it was equipped to receive one, since it had been necessary to slit the leather with a knife under each jaw of the opening and insert the lock's iron mandible through the two slits and clash it home; so that any other hand with a similar knife could have cut the whole lock from the pouch as easily as it had been clasped to it" (p. 12). But though the lock is of little practical value, it is never referred to as meaningless. Its initial symbolic importance is that of a "kind of landmark." The particular meaning of the lock is not explicitly defined until a few pages later, when it has become an irrevocable part of the tie between the settlement and the federal government, through its agent, the rider who delivers the mail:

> So the old lock was not even a symbol of security: it was a gesture of salutation, of free men to free men, of civilization to civilization across not just the three hundred miles of wilderness to Nashville, but the fifteen hundred to Washington: of respect without servility, allegiance without abasement to the government which they had helped to found and had accepted with pride but still as free men, still free to withdraw from it at any moment when the two of them found themselves no longer compatible, the old lock meeting the pouch each time on its arrival, to clasp it in iron and inviolable symbolism. . . . (p. 12)

The situational irony here is that the lock, not only impractical itself but displacing useful food, seed, and powder on its earlier trip from Carolina, comes to mean something more to the settlers than all the practical things in the entire settlement: an expressed desire for continued free federation with the outside order. What follows is the natural consequence of communal self-awareness, the recognition of the need for the establishment of law to protect the community from its own vices.[2]

In Jefferson—or Habersham, as the settlement was originally named—this second acknowledgment occurs by "fortuity . . . chance and accident" (p. 4). A small group of bandits is "captured by chance by an incidental band of civilian more-or-less militia and brought in to the Jefferson jail because it was the nearest one" (p. 5).[3] When the militia and a lynching party begin to contend for possession of the prisoners, the settlement sends a keg of whiskey for them to think on, and waits for all parties to settle down: "then the law-and-order party [Compson, a landowner, Dr. Peabody, Habersham's successor, and Ratcliffe, the post trader] made a rapid sortie and gathered up all the comatose opposition, lynchers and captors too, and dumped them all into the jail with the prisoners and locked the door again . . . " (p. 16). The lock used for incarceration is, of course, the fifteen pound monster lock, transferred from the mail pouch to the door when the bandits were first jailed. The prisoners escape during the night, and the settlement wakes to find "not just the lock gone from the door nor even just the door gone from the jail, but the entire wall gone" (p. 16). Holston demands that his lock be brought back, and Compson and the others find themselves faced with a true dilemma, involving "not the escaped bandits and the aborted reward, but the lock" (p. 17).

The fateful existence of the lock in the settlement was, from the beginning, a consignment of responsibility to the principle of law. The lock now hopelessly lost, the people understand that some reparation must be made, though no one knows how to make it. The problem then, is *what to do with the responsibility for the lock*. It is of little significance that they owe the cost of the lock to old Alec Holston, its original owner. He will not accept the cash equivalent but demands the lock itself. Holston—and the community eventually recognizes this—is demanding the restoration of the principle for which the lock stands in some other objectification of law. The solutions proposed by Ratcliffe are helpful in clarifying the point. The people could not charge the lock to the United States Government subsidy for the Chickasaw tribe moving to Oklahoma, because it was the lock itself which represented honorable agreement with that government. This, Ratcliffe's first suggestion, is accepted at first without much consideration because, at the time, the people are more preoccupied with "their own moderation, since they wanted nothing—least of all, to escape any just blame—but a fair and decent adjustment of the lock" (pp. 21–22).

Fair and decent Ratcliffe's suggestion is. But it is not a *responsible* solution. And though the money is fair payment on the debt, monetary recompense itself holds no honor. Initially the contest here is to see who can get the community to pay *him* the money, and the way to win is to have the most conscience-easing excuse. But eventually the settlers come to see that they are collectively responsible for the lock and that its significance is not purchasable. The second proposition is to rest five-hundred dollars with Holston until a new lock can be made in Carolina. This is foiled by Thomas Jefferson Pettigrew, the mail carrier, who states infallibly that the U.S. Post Office owned the lock ever since it had been clasped on the mail pouch and thereby donated to the government. To support his argument Pettigrew flawlessly quotes the mail-tampering laws; and though Compson thinks Pettigrew wants only confusion and Ratcliffe is convinced his aim is money, Peabody at last discerns that he wants neither, but something far more important: a place in history. It is Peabody who later tells Pettigrew that by building three walls instead of one for the jail, they will have "another four-wall house. That will be the courthouse" (p. 28). In a kind of offhand comment he also tells Pettigrew that the town will be named for him, albeit by his middle name, Jefferson.

It is important to understand that the naming is not a payoff to Pettigrew to forget about the lock. The point is that what Pettigrew wanted was *bona fide* recognition as a member of the community for whom he performs the service of delivering the mail as a kind of federal sanction of their incorporation. The town responds with highest honors, and Pettigrew is duly humbled. In his humility he offers the easier alternative of listing the lock as fifty dollars worth of axel grease on the government Indian subsidy. But Peabody sticks to the name; "We can't ever forget that any more now" (p. 29).

The fury aroused by the lock episode enlightens the entire community to the recognition of its own essential nature. When the settlement of Habersham grew to a certain strength, a certain size, its principle of law outgrew objectification in a lock of even the largest proportions. Justice achieved a stature important enough to warrant its objectification in a full-sized courthouse. With the commitment to build one came the achievement, the status, the condition of township, recognizable and defined by a name.

The problem now was that the structure was hardly a thing to be proud of. It is a lean-to courthouse "which it had taken them almost thirty years not only to realise [sic] they didn't have, but to discover that they hadn't even needed, missed, lacked; and which, before they had owned six months, they discovered was nowhere near enough" (pp. 29–30). The builders of the lean-to pause in the middle of its construction to speak the town's name among themselves, in the aura of "one compound dream-state" (p. 33). Their dreams are of what they hope the town will become, and the courthouse is thus an embodiment of the "town-ness" of Jefferson and the dreams of its inhabitants. Fingering the dimensions of their status as a center of order, the townspeople soon discover, too, that their effort to deal with the bandits has bestowed on the town nothing less than the status of county seat. The courthouse then, is vested with representation of the place as first a town, as the center of justice for the district, and as a collective dwelling with a future.

So a new structure must be designed. Thomas Sutpen's architect is at hand, and the townspeople place a good deal of hope in him: "they— Compson perhaps, Peabody certainly—could imagine him . . . standing in a trackless wilderness dreaming colonnades and porticoes and fountains and promenades in the style of David" (p. 38). This is, of course, Peabody's *image* of the architect. It is an image concocted in the hope that he dreams as they do. At this point in Jefferson's history the settlement is nearly as trackless as Sutpen's Hundred, and the townspeople are hoping the architect can dream them a courthouse in the middle of their wilderness. The dream already conceived in their minds, the people watch the architect stake out the dimensions not only of the courthouse, but of a grove to enclose it and an entire town square as well.[4]

As it turns out, of course, the architect is as despotically practical in designing the town square as he was in *Absalom* when he tamed Sutpen's original plan to something less than the size of the town. His most practical contribution is a kiln to make the brick, from which at least four other structures in Jefferson are eventually built: a newer jail, two churches, and a female academy, all embodiments of virtue (i.e., justice, piety and chastity).

No structures built from the architect's kiln are mercantile, except the storefronts, mentioned only at their passing (p. 244).

The Prologue's account of the town's growth from this point on is more historical in its mode than mythical, and it recalls how the courthouse survived when the square was burnt by Federal troops in 1863: "It didn't escape; it simply survived: harder than axes, tougher than fire, more fixed than dynamite; encircled by the tumbled and blackened ruins of lesser walls, it still stood, even the topless smoke-stained columns, gutted of course and roofless, but immune, not one hair even out of the Paris architect's almost forgotten plumb..." (p. 46).

For all his ability to express the quality of endurance in living characters, Faulkner describes perhaps even more successfully an inanimate representation of this, his most cherished value. The degree to which a structure embodies the values of a community determines the extent that it must endure the fiery tests of time and war, fire and flood. It was this kind of test which Holston's lock failed at the time it became insufficient as a token of law. The lock *was* law. But personal liberty, says Faulkner, "and freedom were almost a physical condition like fire and flood" (p. 6), and when the lock failed to restrain the condition of freedom, failed to keep the captors in check, when it was shown the lock could be circumvented, it lost its viability and its validity.

For the people of Jefferson, the courthouse is the container not only of the values professed by the community as a whole, but of all the dreams of all the participants:

> But above all, the courthouse: the center, the focus, the hub... musing, brooding, symbolic and ponderable, tall as cloud, solid as rock, dominating all: protector of the weak, judicate and curb of the passions and lusts, repository and guardian of the aspirations and the hopes.... [B]eing the sum of all, it must raise all of their hopes and aspirations level with its own aspirant and soaring cupola, so that, sweating and tireless and unflagging, they would look about at one another a little shyly, a little amazed, with something like humility too, as if they were realising [*sic*], or were for a moment at least capable of believing, that men, all men, including themselves, were a little better, purer maybe even, than they had thought, expected, or even needed to be. (pp. 40, 41–42)

The courthouse is the statement of the people of Jefferson, *as* Jefferson the community. As a public structure it concretizes not only the single aspiration of the community as a whole, but also the collected aspirations of all its members. Its intention is to be the public enclosure of individual aspirations toward community.

The Snopes Trilogy

The Hamlet: "All This ... Just to Eat and Sleep In"

Sartoris is the embodiment of a communal leader's dream of communal order. It is the embodiment of the way of life which goes on within it, a manner of living which supports communal life and makes cultural achievement possible. Sutpen's Hundred is a private design to embody personal worth. It not only subordinates communal responsibility to dynastic achievement but presents image, not history or substance, as the evidence of such achievement.

The Old Frenchman Place is the remnant of a dream. It is what remains when there is not enough of a community to support the dream, or progeny to perpetuate it. As a result the dream and its name dissolve to oblivion and are forgotten. But the house still embodies an aura of past elegance, which Flem Snopes employs in *The Hamlet* to deceive even the wily Ratliff.

The mansion of the Huguenot Louis Grenier, one of Jefferson's three original pioneers, is still standing at the turn of the century as the Snopes trilogy opens. Though by this time his name has long since been forgotten in *The Hamlet*, the greater part of his legend is recounted in *Requiem for a Nun*. At the time of the naming of Jefferson, Grenier had already established his place on a section of the north bank of the Yoknapatawpha River, at what comes to be known as Frenchman's Bend, the Old Frenchman Place: "his plantation, his manor, his kitchens and stables and kennels and fields which a hundred years later will have vanished, his name and his blood too, leaving nothing but the name of his plantation and his own fading corrupted legend ... " (p. 33).

Of the five legendary plantations in the county, the Old Frenchman Place is most comparable to Sutpen's Hundred. A principal difference in the catalogs of both is the mention of kitchens at Grenier's and smokehouses at Sutpen's. Though Ellen Coldfield's presence brings a certain feminine softness to Sutpen's Spartan existence, Grenier's kitchens indicate the presence of, if not a Mistress of the Manor, certainly a more delicate cuisine. Meanwhile, the mention of kennels at Grenier's recalls that Sutpen has no need of them, since his Negroes track his game, including his French architect, who certainly could have suggested kennels had there been any need for them.

The reasons for Grenier's demise are obscure, though what is known about him is referred to as a legend. Of Faulkner's other planters, John Sartoris (though certainly not a legend in his own time) is given larger-than-life stature through Bayard's mythical rendering. The events of Sutpen's life become his legend as they are told and retold within the novel *Absalom, Absalom!*, the document of that legend. But where Sutpen's is the legend of a corrupted man, Grenier's is a "fading corrupted legend."[1] The suggestion is that the life behind it was honorable enough, but that lacking living progeny to maintain a living past, the details have decayed with time.

The legend of the house as it now stands in *The Hamlet*, the dream it contains, is of buried treasure; "gold which the builder was reputed to have buried somewhere about the place when Grant came through the country on his Vicksburg campaign."[2]

By the turn of the century the dream still has not reached any particular intensity among the inhabitants of Frenchman's Bend. The present owner of the house in *The Hamlet* is Will Varner, who is more puzzled by the impracticality of spaciousness than awed by any sense of "fallen baronial splendor" it might still possess. "I'm trying to find out what it must have felt like to be the fool that would need all this," he says, "just to eat and sleep in" (p. 6). His motive for buying the house in the first place is never disclosed, but his reason for keeping it is its lesson in frugality: "I reckon I'll keep what there is left of it, just to remind me of my one mistake. This is the only thing I ever bought in my life I couldn't sell to nobody" (p. 6).

Varner does sell it later, of course, to Flem Snopes, who is obviously aware of the legend of buried gold, and has a plan to make his own profit from it. In Flem's transaction with Ratliff and Armstid the dream-legend is more active than ever before because Grenier's legend has, with time, acquired the power of an Eldorado myth. Flem's ability to wield its entire blinding illusion of quick riches, combined with Ratliff's momentary and Armstid's permanent loss of the careful balance of pride and humility, open the way for the success of Snopes's venture.

The legend of the Old Frenchman Place is vested with the trappings of its historical time. Ratliff's head is spinning with a vision of the Old Order as he and Bookwright drive up to the old mansion by way of the old lane, "where thirty years ago a courier...had galloped with the news of Sumter, where perhaps the barouche had moved, the women swaying and pliant in hooped crinoline beneath parasols, the men in broadcloth riding the good horses at the wheels, talking about it..." (pp. 342–43). Even the fact that the names are forgotten contributes to the sacrosanct nature of the entry vista up the long road: "Now the scar ran straight as a plumb-line along a shaggy hedgerow of spaced cedars decreed there by the same nameless architect who had planned and built the house for its nameless master" (p. 343). With their ownership of the house secured, the three men spend two nights digging and two days sleeping before Ratliff recovers his quick thinking. If it seems difficult to suppose that Ratliff could go awry for so long, it should be remembered that the trio eats and sleeps within the old house itself, submerged in the aura which suspends its legend: "The room they chose had a fourteen-foot ceiling. There were the remains of a once-gilt filigree of cornice above the gutted windows and the ribbed and serrated grin of lathing from which the plaster had fallen and the skeleton of another prismed chandelier" (p. 364). The collection of corporeal terms here (remains, ribbed, grin, skeleton) suggests again that this is the body of a house whose spirit (but not aura) has fled.

These images of the Old Order's past grandeur and their transformation into the dream of quick riches are all that remain of the *genius loci* of the Old Frenchman Place. Whatever communal values it once fostered have decayed, and the value of the property, its practical value in dollars, has been inflated in false dreams.

The remainder of the Snopes Trilogy's fictive architecture, including the town house of Manfred de Spain, is almost all related in one degree or another to the rise of Flem Snopes. Despite the strenuous existential struggle of Jack Houston to find his place in the world, there is little of his condition that Faulkner does not specifically express in effort rather than edifice. The only other great house in the proximity of Frenchman's Bend (and for that matter in Yoknapatawpha County)[3] is the mansion of Cassius de Spain, the most specifically influential house-as-image in the Yoknapatawpha canon. Though it appears only in the short story "Barn Burning," De Spain's mansion and its story were originally an opening chapter of *The Hamlet*.[4] The Major's home is not only an excellent piece of fictive architecture, but also has implications toward Manfred de Spain's town house and other built forms of the trilogy.

The rural farm of Cassius de Spain is the last place Abner Snopes is seen sharecropping before he is found on Varner's place in the opening scenes of *The Hamlet*. The farm is nearly impossible to place on the Yoknapatawpha map. That Snopes comes from De Spain's to farm at Varner's suggests the Major's place is in the southeast quadrant of the county, or at least in the south half. That De Spain owns the hunting camp on the Tallahatchie is of no matter, since it does not require that he live nearby. Also, "Barn Burning" is set twelve or thirteen years after De Spain has quit hunting and sold the timber rights to the area around the camp. In "The Bear," McCaslin, Sam Fathers and Tennie's Jim must "drive away to Jefferson, to join Major de Spain" (GDM, p. 169), indicating that De Spain's place is close to Jefferson, perhaps even between the McCaslin place and the town, in the northeast quadrant of the county.

Location is less important, though, since the architecture is the influential element in the formative experience of Ab's young son, Colonel Sartoris Snopes.[5] Sarty's first view of De Spain's house comes as he walks with his overbearing father to see their new landlord. The events of the previous day— Harris's suit, the near-necessity of having to testify, the scuffle outside the store and his father's reprimand—have put Sarty in a precarious tension between the demands of his envious Snopes blood and his innate sense of justice and right order. The demands of his nature as a Snopes are objectified physiologically in the blood which flows in his veins and affirmed by his father's vengeful instruction. His sense of justice, however, his innate sense of the right and the good, which he knows to be better than his blood, has no such objectification, no *thing* to affirm that what he feels strongest is indeed true. The thing which fills this need, the objectification and affirmation of his sense of right order, is the De Spain mansion, and the boy's first view of it links it to his sense of justice and gives him the strength of his convictions.

What gives De Spain's house the power to embody the boy's flowering notion of the right order of things is the uniqueness of its image: "for all the twelve movings, they had sojourned until now in a poor country, a land of small farms and fields and houses, and he had never seen a house like this before" (p. 10).[6] Having never seen a manor house Sarty associates De Spain's with the only other edifice associated with the truth, and so ties it to the order of justice: "*Hit's big as a courthouse,*" he says. For the moment his terror and despair, the source of which is his father, disappear and are replaced "with a surge of peace and joy" (p. 10), the result of visual contact with a concretization of his own feelings.

The quality which impresses both Ab and Sarty is the whiteness of the house and of all its details. The rug is pale, the chandeliers glitter and the gold frames, presumably of mirrors or portraits, gleam. All this elegance moves Ab only to envy its owner and the control with which he can maintain its whiteness. But Sarty reponds with no such feelings, even when bombarded with whiteness as he charges the house to warn De Spain. The boy runs "up the drive toward the lighted house, the lighted door," sees first "the Negro in the linen jacket," then "the white man too emerging from a white door down the hall" (p. 23). The quality of these exterior and interior elements serves only to support the cause to which Sarty has now attached himself in his effort to protect part of its associative architecture from Snopes arson.

Cassius de Spain has a more conscious understanding of his home as the embodiment of a lived way of life than others of his stature, and he fiercely defends it in the "Barn Burning" story. But the chronology of De Spain's built and unbuilt property is a revealing thread in the history of the architectural dissolution of Yoknapatawpha seen in the last two-thirds of the Snopes

Trilogy, a dissolution from the meaningful life of the rural manor house to the artificial respectability of town house facades.

In 1885 (the year Sarty is born) De Spain begins his divestiture by leasing timber rights to the wilderness. When Ike McCaslin is twenty-one (1888), De Spain offers him a room in his house, possibly his rural one, though Cassius seems already to have the "big wooden house," Manfred's "ancestral home" in town. When Abner Snopes burns the De Spain barn in 1895, Manfred, who would be about eighteen, does not appear in the story, though it will be three years before he fights in the Spanish-American War. Finally, by 1909, in *The Town*, Cassius is dead, and Manfred is "living alone in his late father's big wooden house with a cook and a houseman in a white coat" (*The Town*, p. 14). As Flem Snopes aims toward Jefferson through a chain of architectural enclosures in Frenchman's Bend, the concretizations of what Grenier, Sartoris, De Spain, and the later McCaslin stand for begin to fade from the landscape.

The progress of Flem Snopes from tenant to bank president can be marked by a hierarchy of places of which he is given custody. Though Varner's tenant farm is rented to Ab and not Flem, it is where Varner first sees Flem (*The Hamlet*, p. 22). The changes in Flem's station present a movement from subservience to near autonomy, ending in a kind of corulership of the area with Will Varner.

He is first the clerk in Varner's store, which he tends so conscienciously as to charge even its owner, Varner himself, for his own merchandise.[7] By fall of the same year (1897) Flem lives in the village, and in September Jody is told to stay in the store while Flem tends the wagon scales in the cotton gin.

The clerk of a store as small and remote as that at Varner's Crossroads has no financial power or authority, except perhaps to validate the price of merchandise; and the only duty of this station is to accept the money for the goods purchased. Flem has managed to exercise this power to its limit and beyond, enforcing payment from the store's owner and enforcing it outside the store.

When Flem moves from the store to the cotton gin, he sits "on the stool behind the scale-beam" (p. 59). This is a seat of some authority. It requires the recording of a measurement of ginned cotton, the basis on which payment is made. The move is both a displacement of Jody and the assumption of Jody's authority. While a clerk at the store, Flem was merely filling in a position which leaves both owner and son free to do other things. The watchers on the gallery (and the whole community) assume that Jody sends Flem to superintend the opening of the gin as the delegation of a lesser task. The delegator then "gets to" sit in the store. But in fact Flem goes there because he has been delegated the *authority* to sit behind the scales, while Jody has been *demoted* as clerk, by whom no one seems to know. Later still this same year, while Varner makes "his yearly settlement with his tenants and debtors" (p. 61), Flem sits on a nail keg at his knee. Varner still holds the cash box here, sitting at the desk, but Flem holds the books. Though Will still manages the money, it may be said that he is merely the cashier now, while Flem is the accountant.

"At the next harvest"[8] Flem not only sits "at the gin scales," but sits alone at Will's desk as well, "with the cash from the sold crops and the account books before him" (p. 90). He is now the sole authority of the settlement's meager economic existence. He has moved from stool to nail keg to desk chair.

The story of Flem's success in Frenchman's Bend has many things to say about dwelling in a place—things which may help explain the novel. To begin with, it is not long after Flem begins to clerk in the store when it is said that he now lives in the village. Though this verb precludes a descriptive account of his appearance in the church life of the settlement, the account ends with Flem now "boarded and lodged" with a family nearby. There are some distinctions necessary here. That Flem now "live[s] in the village" is not to say he dwells there. To lodge is a specifically temporary kind of living and suggests only a place to eat and sleep, a shared table and bed. The community knows that Flem is attempting to gain an existential foothold. They all know, too, that the goal of his acquisitiveness, the last move, will be to occupy Varner's house.

It is interesting to suppose that Bookwright's comment, "Anyhow, he aint moved into Varner's house yet" (p. 58), refers not to the Old Frenchman's Place but to a farm mentioned later, "another place which Varner owned and kept himself as his home farm" (p. 62). It is only fifteen minutes from the store (p. 244). Varner certainly does not dwell at the Old Frenchman's house. He has no guests there and does not even sit on the portico but on the lawn in front of the house. If Flem is aiming for the Old Frenchman's Place, he does so to unseat Varner as lord of his province. If his sights are on Varner's home, he is seeking to displace him as a dweller in the community. Such a basic attack, however, would presuppose sophisticated motives which Flem acquires only later in *The Town* (respectability as a member of the community). Not until this second novel will Flem reach for both economic and domestic seats and achieve them simultaneously by ousting Manfred de Spain from his bank and his home as well. The ambiguity of reference remains, however, especially when the second mention of Flem's apparent goal occurs *after* we are told specifically that it is Varner's home farm on which Flem pastures his herd of Herefords.

By the time the final goal is mentioned again ("that just leaves Will's house" [p. 71]), the dwellings and possessions of all the principals have been catalogued. Flem lodges at a house a mile from Varner's Crossroads. Varner dwells at his homestead farm and reigns from his barrel chair on the lawn of

Figure 7-1. Detail of Varner's Crossroads and Frenchman's Bend

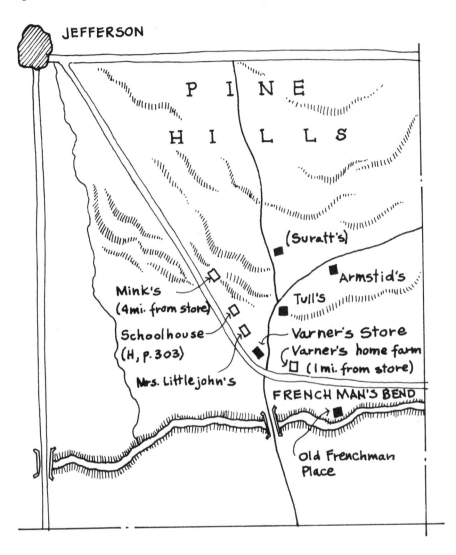

JEFFERSON

P I N E

H I L L S

(Suratt's)

Armstid's

Mink's
(4mi. from store)

Tull's

Schoolhouse
(H, p. 303)

Varner's Store
Varner's home farm
(1mi. from store)

Mrs. Littlejohn's

FRENCH MAN'S BEND

Old Frenchman
Place

the Old Frenchman's Place. Ratliff owns a house in Jefferson and is half owner of a restaurant there. Despite these possessions, Ratliff is never seen in his house except while recuperating from his gall-bladder ailment. It is mentioned that his widowed sister keeps this house for him, but it can hardly be said that he dwells there. At first glance, Ratliff's conditions with respect to the bed and the table seem as alarmingly tenuous as Flem Snopes's. Yet, in his transient way, Ratliff seems to be at home anywhere he is. He dines either at his restaurant in Jefferson, a hundred yards from the gallery at Varner's Crossroads, or shares a table with clients on his route. Flem boards. Ratliff is given a bed wherever he is invited. Flem lodges. Ratliff dwells everywhere, anywhere he is. Flem dwells nowhere. He has bed and table for a fee and pays it in hopes of gaining an existential foothold in the community. Flem is never seen in the act of dwelling, only in the act of carrying his new straw suitcase into Varner's home.

If the question is, "Where does Ratliff dwell?", the answer is that he dwells in the condition of itinerancy. His home is his buckboard, or for that matter, anywhere he is invited: "He could have passed from table to table in that country for six months without once putting his hand into his pocket" (p. 55). He may be said, then, to dwell not only in Jefferson, but in the entire county, even in the four counties encompassed by his route. It is this entire area to which he belongs, and he dwells there not by virtue of ownership but by existential condition of belonging. His territory is not a vague, characterless space but a skein of *places*, each with a distinct character given it by the people who dwell there and are known to him through his interaction with them. To dwell is to inhabit the world. Man dwells when he is able to concretize the world in buildings and things, and Ratliff does this through his tales. In that he is a seer and a maker, he may also be called poet,[9] and his tales are composed of the history of the district and the meaning of its places.

Ratliff's most poignant remark—his advice to Bookwright and Tull as inhabitants of Frenchman's Bend faced with the danger of Snopesism—is made as they eat in Ratliff's restaurant in Jefferson:

> "Aint none of you folks out there done nothing about it?" he said.
> "What could we do?" Tull said. "It aint right. But it aint none of our business."
> "I believe I would think of something if I lived there," Ratliff said.

Bookwright goes on to explain the real reason, the real threat: "'And wind up with one of them bow ties in place of your buckboard and team...'" (p. 72). "Living there," living in a place, requires, demands at times, defending the place against challenges and even risking the place itself to defend meaningful existence there. The disinclination to take up a challenge to Snopes is based on the fear of losing those things with and in which we dwell.

The episode with the goats which follows the discussion in the restaurant is Ratliff's attempt to *do* something; and he is very possibly risking his buckboard and team by challenging Snopes's invasion into the domain for which Ratliff, as one who dwells in the district, feels at least partially responsible. His effort is of the same temper as John Sartoris's act of ousting the Burdens from Jefferson: he wishes to save the community from immanent disorder. Though it is somewhat expected of him, John Sartoris's act is heroic, first because he succeeds, and second because he responds sooner than expected. Ratliff's effort is heroic because it is more than is expected of him and because it is undertaken almost too late, when the community has already begun to ask what can be done. Though he achieves a modicum of success, his effort becomes moot as Flem strides on to greater things in Jefferson.

The Town: "Miniature of Men's Passions and Hopes"

Only much later, in *The Mansion*, is Ratliff seen dwelling almost exclusively in Jefferson, "living alone in the cleanest little house you ever saw" (p. 206). His preoccupation with Jefferson is, of course, his continuing watch of Snopeses and of Flem's rise to bank presidency.

These last two novels of the trilogy[10] are more about town life than town space, but the two primary movements—the vertical rise of Flem and the steady horizontal effort of Mink—are expressed in terms of built form and natural element. Flem's story is depicted in banks and houses and their interiors and furnishings; Mink's is in terms of natural forces, natural places, and the elemental earth.

Flem's procession from Varner's store to gin to blacksmith shop to old mansion makes its leap to Jefferson by his attainment of Ratliff's part of the restaurant in the town. From here the chain of structures he gets charge of is somewhat parallel to that at Varner's Crossroads. Initially he achieves complete control of a place of provisioning (first Varner's store, now the Jefferson restaurant). He then moves to an architectural engine of some sort, gin or power plant. Despite Chick Mallison's implication that the new superintendent has complete control over Jefferson's water and electricity (both very basic elements), Flem cannot use his new position this way any more than he could use Varner's gin to such purpose. Rather, he will use the financial content of the position to again gain a seat at the knee of the town's fiscal baron, as he did in *The Hamlet*. Flem's move to vice-president and then to president of the bank is a parallel to his move from the store nail keg to old Will's desk.

Since it is about this time that Flem buys the house he had previously been renting, the question arises again as to whether he dwells there. It is the same "small rented house in a back street near the edge of town" (T, p. 9) in which he lives as restaurateur and as plant superintendent. But the important point about Snopes's habitations (small house or refurbished mansion) is that, though he and his family live there, no home life is depicted in them. What there is of embodied meaning in the dwellings of these two novels is not engendered by Flem Snopes. Like the image of respectability he seeks, the interior furnishings of the house he inhabits are the *picture* of upright community living without the substance, the lived life behind it. Later Flem, like Thomas Sutpen, will seek the image of a house rather than the embodiment of a home.

After Chick Mallison's brief mention of the wisteria arbor in the side yard of the Snopes house, the first real detail of the house is from Gavin Stevens's view of its interior when he visits Eula. The objects and the furniture of the sitting room remind Gavin of a picture, a photograph "reproduced in color in a wholesale furniture catalogue" (T, p. 221). Eula's recounting of the trip to Memphis is a peeling away of the veneers to reveal Flem's true motive. The salesman first suggests the image of ambition. Then, knowing the image desired is not one of wealth ("Not expensive"), he suggests success, then family heritage. When Flem rejects all these, the salesman calls in his wife, who "reads" Flem and understands his motivation to be more than all the previous ones, yet somehow inexpressible. The best Gavin can do is to describe it as "that furniture catalogue picture ... scaled ... down to that one which Flem holds imperative that the people of Yoknapatawpha County must have of him" (T, p. 224). Flem wants furniture which speaks not of wealth, success or long family heritage—in *The Mansion* we are told that Flem "traded in Major de Spain's mother's furniture for it" (M, p. 215)—but which elicits general respect from the people of Jefferson. Flem's furniture is a part of his striving for respectability, and exhibits the same wrong choice of image over action which characterized Sutpen's building effort. The point is clear when Ratliff says, "Call it civic virtue" (T, p. 175). Respect is earned from virtuous action. But when virtue is misunderstood as a quality already possessed instead of the active practice of good habit, it is possible to assume that acknowledgment of and respect for virtue can be generated from objects symbolic of virtue.[11] Flem's furniture is certainly not that of a virtuous leader, nor does he pretend that it is, because "Only a fool would try to fool smart people" (T, p. 222). In its scaled-down form, the furniture is only the image, the picture of what virtuous action might earn a civic leader. Given no evidence to the contrary, Jefferson must accept the picture as evidence of the man.

Gavin is the only visitor to this interior who is recorded in the novel. During his talk with Eula, he notes the presence of a table and even a hearthfire in their house, but despite the impression that Flem acquires his furniture for the perusal of the entire town, there are no other accounts of visitors or their impressions.

The Mansion: "Respectability's Virgin Matterhorn"

Flem's move from his smaller house to De Spain's is a shift from internal (and somewhat intimate) images of respectability to one large external one, the interior of which, according to Ratliff, is never seen by anyone except Flem's cook and the yardman (though of course Gavin will see it many times). The first five notations of Manfred's town house refer to it as "[Manfred's] father's big wooden house" (T, p. 14), "Manfred de Spain's old home" (T, p. 347), his "birthsite" (T, p. 348), "De Spain's rejuvenated ancestral home" (M, p. 141), and the house Manfred "was born in" (M, p. 152). Whether or not old Cassius owned both a rural farm and this town house in the trilogy, this one is certainly Manfred's birthplace. The original house is definitely not a showcase home: it is, as Ratliff says, "jest a house: two storey, with a gallery for Major de Spain, Manfred's paw, to set on when he wasn't fishing or hunting or practising a little law ... " (M, p. 153). [12] The significance of its remodeling is spoken quite unambiguously by Ratliff:

> the house the folks owning the money would see Manfred de Spain walk into ever evening after he locked the money up and went home, wouldn't be enough for Flem Snopes. The house they would see him walk into ever evening ... would have to be the physical symbol of all them generations of respectability and aristocracy that not only would a been too proud to mishandle other folks' money, but couldn't possibly ever needed to. (M, p. 153)

As bank vice-president Flem has no need for the trust the townspeople give to someone whose ancestry and lineage they know. But as bank president he does need that trust; and without a known ancestry, all he can do is emphasize (or exaggerate) its representation. As Ratliff so clearly states, however, "it was jest the house that was altered and transmogrified and symbolised: not him. The house he disappeared into ... might a been the solid aristocratic ancestral symbol of Alexander Hamilton ..., but the feller the owners of that custodianed money seen going and coming out of it was the same one they had done got accustomed to for twenty years now ... (M, pp. 154–55)." [13]

The Snopes remodeling of the De Spain house is a fictional event also participating in the larger architectural history of the age. Flem's transmogrification of the house is a movement from representative symbolic architecture to the overt use of symbolic forms to dignify his house and so lend repectability to his person. His work is part of the misapplication of symbolic forms which led to and precipitated the general loss of symbolization in architecture in the entire western world during the late nineteenth and early twentieth centuries. *The Mansion* and its most prominent theme are part of the literary tradition depicting, in Richard Gill's words, "the decline of the aristocracy in a world of rising tradesmen and parvenus." [14]

Most of the details of this remodeling are significant in themselves. The major modification to the house consists in "tearing off Major de Spain's front gallery and squaring up the back of the house and building and setting up them colyums to reach all the way from the ground up to the second-storey roof" (M, p. 154). Without any references to a portico, the novel seems to suggest that the columns are installed all the way across the front, in a colonnade such as might be seen in Belle Mina in Alabama. The change from gallery to columnated stylobate is a change in the character of the house from quiet leisure to imposing formality. Where the old Major just wants a place to "set" on his gallery when he's not fishing or hunting, Flem is only concerned with the facade his investors see him going into at night. The facade is so imposing that even Linda will not go inside when she drives her father over to watch its progress. [15]

Linda's aversion seems to be as much for the person of her father as for his house. The parlor where she receives her formal visitors (like the two Finns) is "diagonally across the hall from the room where old Snopes was supposed to spend all his life that didn't take place in the bank" (M, p. 222). Her sitting room is both diagonally across and upstairs from Flem's room in the rear. Assuming the plan is the standard central hall with flanking rooms, Linda's is the upstairs right front room. This is the intimate place where Linda and Gavin meet and talk. The stairs to this room know Gavin's feet as the doorknobs and sills of Sutpen's place know Henry's touch, and the sitting room knows him too (M, p. 423). The room has a hearth and a mantel "where they transacted all her business which required communication between them" (M, p. 426). This is the mantel which Gavin describes as that "which she had designed at the exact right height and width to support a foolscap pad" (M, p. 237). It would otherwise be of little note but for the fact that it compares so favorably with the mantel in Flem's room at the diagonal opposite of the house. This room is furnished with "another swivel chair like the one in the bank" (M, p. 155), but the detail most remarked, especially by Ratliff, is "that hand-carved hand-painted Mount Vernon mantelpiece" (M, p. 156), accurately explicated by V.K. as "what you might call respectability's virgin Matterhorn" (M, p. 158). [16] The two mantels are juxtaposed as Gavin follows Linda upstairs to talk of Mink's release from prison:

> following her through the hall at the end of which was the door to the room where her father...sat...with his feet propped on the unpainted wooden ledge he had had his Frenchman's Bend carpenter-kinsman nail at the proper height across the Adam mantel; on up the stairs and...in to her sitting room whose mantel had been designed to the exact height for them to stand before while he used the foolscap pad and pencil which was its fixture.... (M, p. 366)

Flem's unpainted ledge is respectability's accommodation to comfort, convenience. Like the one at the bank, it is merely a place to put his feet "between foreclosures" (M, p. 227). Linda's mantel is the place where she and Gavin discuss their most intimate business, designed "so that she could read the words as my hand formed them," Gavin says, "like speech, almost like hearing" (M, p. 237). That is, Linda's mantel has to do with the head, communication, and speech. Flem's has to do with the feet and inactivity, with stasis.

The room in which Mink finds Linda, however, is not this upstairs room (though he has heard of it) but the front left downstairs room, "walled almost to the ceiling with more books than he knew existed" (M, p. 413). This is the room in front of Flem's and across the hall from the parlor. From his waiting place next to the hedge, Mink sees the servants leave and then peers in one of the side windows of Flem's room. He begins to go around the rear of the house to see if Linda's room—which he knows is diagonally upstairs—is lit, but decides instead to check the room in front of Flem's (which has its lights on). At the moment he sees Linda, several previously undisclosed factors come into play.

Mink has not actually been around the back of the house, and so he still does not know for certain where the back door is, though he has seen the servants come from behind the house to leave by the side gate. His uncertainty also indicates that he has no familiarity with this typical manor house plan, which always has a door at the rear of the hall. If Linda sits with her back to the hall door, as Mink notes, she must be facing the window through which he is looking. As attentive to her reading as she is, it is still surprising that she does not see him looking in the window.

It is part of Mink's position as Flem's angel of death that he need not sneak into this house the back way but can enter through the front door, "like any other guest, visitor, caller" (M, p. 415). Teleology has taken over here, and no one can say Mink is unwelcome. As Flem turns to meet his execution, he must take his feet from their resting place and place them on the floor. He does not stand up, but his feet must perforce leave the floor again as Mink's hard-won ammunition strikes home.

It is because Mink's progress must continue ever forward that he seeks an exit out the back of the house and finds "the other door in the wall beyond the chair" (M, p. 416). Linda guides him away from this closet door to his true exit out the back. Though the closet door has no particular importance in the story, it is uproariously ironic that Flem locks his closet but leaves his front door open to his final nemesis. The few difficulties Mink has encountered on the way to the house have been overcome with work and faith. The only real obstacle he encounters now is this locked door on his way out.

Beyond V.K. Ratliff's perceptive and witty remarks on the Snopes—*né* De Spain—mansion, its overall significance is articulated in two pages of *The Mansion* which compare the Backus plantation as redone by Melisandre's late husband to Flem's monstrosity. Rose Hill, it is said, has been "transmogrified by the New Orleans gangster's money as old Snopes had tried to do to the De Spain house with his Yoknapatawpha County gangster's money and failed since here the rich and lavish cash had been spent with taste so that you didn't really see it at all but merely felt it, breathed it, like warmth or temperature..." (M, p. 358). Though Harriss has many more acres to work with, he has apparently done it "with taste," where "the cold mausoleum in which old Snopes had immolated that much of his money" was done "without grace or warmth" (M, p. 359).[17] No one would have expected more from Snopes, but comparing the two places, despite their great difference of scale, reveals a much more important point: all the other manor houses of the trilogy (or, for that matter, of Yoknapatawpha) are great landed things, surrounded by many acres. Flem's house, though it has the plan and façade of a mansion, is by the demands of its site a town house with no manor to authenticate its form—no manor, that is, unless Flem considers the town to be his plantation. And this seems to be precisely so, at least in the figurative sense, from his manipulation of people and cultivation of the town's financial crop. Hardly concerned about the political or social order of this community except in its appearance, he is in no way a patriarch of his "estate."

Having explored the possibility that Flem Snopes might be considered, however grudgingly, a dweller in Jefferson, we must settle the question of whether or not he finds his house meaningful. The house seems to be for him something in which he has invested much money—something which carries the mask of his respectability before the town—or a place to sit "between foreclosures." But though it is the place which holds the room where Flem spends "all of his life," nothing of any particular significance to him (save his death) happens within it. His bed is mentioned and of course the mantel, but though there must be a hearth beneath it, no fire is ever seen there. The last piece of furniture he actively uses is the swivel chair like the one at the bank. He dies in the business furniture which is his element. Eventually the entire mansion is returned, through Linda's efforts, to relatives of its original owner.

8

Go Down, Moses

"The Concrete Indication of His Own Vanity's Boundless Conceiving"

The plantation mansion within its cluster of *garçonnières,* smokehouses, and stables and the courthouse within its town square are built forms which share the double station of individual as well as collective significance. Townhouses are individual pieces with more equal relationships among their own kind and among clusters of related structures. In larger urban clusters this relationship is called a neighborhood, but in the Southern small town the entire town has the social homogeneity of a district: the whole town is one neighborhood. Two other building types complete the spectrum from public or social to private or individual—the church and the dog-trot cabin.

Yoknapatawpha churches are what churches are everywhere, gathering places for congregations, sacred spaces where a community assembles in the belief that God will manifest Himself, render Himself available, perhaps even dwell. But Faulkner's churches always seem to be in difficult circumstances, with congregation or structure in near dissolution, in which the practice of faith becomes genuinely heroic and the working of grace particularly strenuous. Compared to others in the Yoknapatawpha canon, Brother Fortinbride's church in *The Unvanquished* is fortunate to have its structure intact. It is an Episcopal church, with pews and a gallery for the Negroes. It is the regular church for the Sartorises, and Doctor Worsham used to be its minister.

After three years of war, all is changed. Though the church still stands, the congregation is now principally hill country people of unknown denominations, in "the first church with a slave gallery some of them had ever seen" (p. 153), and led by the Methodist Brother Fortinbride. As desperate circumstances call for desperate measures, the principal business of the church's ragtag congregation is not prayer (though prayer is its *first* business), but distribution of goods to the poor. In keeping with the upended circumstances which war has brought to this community, the book used for these "services" is an account book, by which Rosa Millard metes out the goods and requires an accounting of their use. Despite the strictness of her charity, Rosa's provision is not unappreciated, and the same congregation comes in from the hills later to attend her funeral.

A church of more precarious structure is Reverend Whitfield's in "Shingles for the Lord." Though it begins needing only a new roof, Res Grier manages to incinerate the place in his attempt to beat Quick at dog trading. Though the point of the story is rendered well and the instructive words of the boy narrator and Whitfield are clear enough, the church itself and its enclosure of sacred space embody much of its meaning. The stop-action tableau of Res and his son suspended over the exploding fire is, of course, an image of the threat of perdition. The nightshirt is the garment of the church's *genius loci*, which it wears in its ascension to the heavens as the dissolving church loses the substance which holds its character as a place.

The simile with which Res Grier's son describes Whitfield's stance is deliciously ambiguous; "what hadn't ought to been created" refers neither to Res Grier nor the church, but to the trouble a man can get himself into when he tries to be something more than "jest a average hard-working farmer trying to do the best he can" (p. 31).[1] Whitfield feels no need "to take his hat off in any presence" (p. 41), despite the fact that it appears the powers of Hell have destroyed his church and driven its spirit from the place. Whitfield knows what Grier's son sees in the red and fading core of the church's shell: that the fire and flood and destruction of men's worst efforts, accident or no, cannot subdue the resilient *genius loci* of a meaningful place. Though it has temporarily ascended to the stars, it will return again to this sacred space when the community rebuilds its enclosure.

The church in *Intruder in the Dust* known as Caledonia Chapel, though it has a less active role than others, is a strong backdrop and has a definite pervading *genius loci* which generates a kind of mysteriousness that is both carnal and sacred. Though Chick Mallison defines various churches by giving them imperative verbs like "Peace [be with you]" and "Repent," "this one said simply: Burn . . . " (*Intruder*, p. 157).[2] Its quiet but still dominant character is expressed in its color and stance. Its weathered gray color is reflected in the granite headstones in its yard, and it rises up like the "high strong constant shaggy pines" among which it stands. Both the headstones and the pines are slightly tilted, and the stones by their color show that they belong to the church, "as if they had been hacked out of its flank with axes" (p. 157). Together these three elements—chapel, headstone, and tree—generate the character of the place and maintain its sacrality against the forensic business which must now be performed there.

In *The Mansion* are two churches, one which falls with seemingly divine wrath on the escaped convict Stillwell, allowing Mink to be freed from prison, and the other a dream of the diasporatic Reverend Goodyhay, which though it still struggles to be built, is already dispensing its grace in allowing Mink the money and transportation to be about his fated business.

If something need be said about all these churches, it is that they are, even in collapse, definitive of themselves. They are enclosures intended for the implementation of grace, in whatever concrete form it may need to take—the necessities of food, clothing, money, transportation, or just plain wisdom. All are generated against overwhelming odds, usually as the result of communal action in a crisis.

The dog-trot cabin is both an archetype of its own and a functional parti for larger domestic building forms. The description of its structure given by Andrew Lytle in his contribution to *I'll Take My Stand*, a part of his consideration of the Southern farmer as a type, is definitive:

> The house is a dog-run with an ell running to the rear, the kitchen and dining-room being in the ell, if the family does not eat in the kitchen; and the sleepingrooms in the main part of the house. The dog-run is a two- or four-crib construction with an open space between, the whole covered by one roof. The run or trot gets its name from the hounds passing through from the front to the rear. It may or may not have a floor, according to the taste or pride of the occupant. This farmer will have it floored, because his grandfather, as he prospered, closed in the dog-run with doors, making it into a hall; added porches front and rear, weatherboarded the logs, and ceiled the two half-story rooms. . . . The hall is almost bare, but scrubbed clean. At the back is a small stairway leading to the half-story. This is where the boys sleep, in their bachelorhood definitely removed from the girls. To the left is the principal room of the house. The farmer and his wife sleep there in a four-poster . . . the youngest chillurn sleep on pallets made up on the floor.[3]

To Mr. Lytle's account might be added some detail from J. Frazier Smith:

> as soon as times became a little better, he wished to observe the proprieties and to divide the living quarters of the sexes of his large family. Then, too, when relatives and friends came visiting, they necessarily came long distances and had to be housed. On such occasions, the men occupied one side of the "dog-trot" house and the women and children the other, while the dogs belonging to the household and to the visitors occupied the run between, and barked their warnings if any disturbances arose outside. During mild weather the family often ate in the run. If much company came, it was used by the young folk for dancing. So close was the wilderness that, in the absence of the dogs, an occasional oppossum would prowl through the run in search of food; hence the common name "possum-run" for the passageway.[4]

These descriptions of the dog-trot cabin suggest that in its simplicity and rough but hardy craftsmanship it is generally representative of the yeoman farmer's fierce independence and Spartan virtues.[5] Larger meanings than this are resplendent in Faulkner's fictive dog-trots, but it is difficult to study these lesser dwellings in themselves as a type. The iconic integrity of the mansion house is strong enough to demand consideration of the overall house form as meaning. But the significance of the simpler dog-trot house, and of the life within it, is more intricately defused within the house form, its furniture, and its foci, particularly the hearth. Accordingly, an examination of Faulkner's dog-trots soon finds itself on the level of meaningful things in the house: furniture and objects.

The best and most representative of the Yoknapatawpha dog-trots are the MacCallum place of *Sartoris/Flags in the Dust* and "The Tall Men," and the McCaslin dog-run house. The MacCallums are Faulkner's stock and stalwart yeomen, and the small amount of exterior architectural detail about their house is all that attests to its typicality.

In both stories the reader is brought up to the house through the visitor's eyes. Bayard, a welcome guest, notices first "a windless plume of smoke... above the trees," after which "in the rambling wall of the house a window glowed with ruddy invitation across the twilight" (S, p. 308).[6] The investigator who comes unwelcomed to serve his warrant in "The Tall Men" has a far more critical eye as he approaches "through a stout paintless gate in a picket fence, up a broad brick walk between two rows of old shabby cedars, toward the rambling and likewise paintless sprawl of the two-story house in the open hall of which the soft lamplight glowed and the lower story of which as the investigator now perceived, was of logs" (CS, p. 46). In both visions the lamplight is quite mellow, holding an invitation from within the house for Bayard, while the "soft lamplight" in the other story glows hospitably in the open hallway of the MacCallums. The critical adjectives in the short story description ("paintless," "shabby," "rambling"), belong to the investigator's view, and the repetition of "paintless," though accurate, should be understood from Davidson's point of view on New England farms, to be a positive attribute.[7] The weathered finish of the log house reflects the character of those who dwell in it—including Buddy's boys who, though their paperwork for service to country is incomplete, are nevertheless more sturdily built and better prepared for the task than most of those whose boots are shined before they enlist.

The house in both stories has a gallery or veranda, paintless in "The Tall Men" and certainly so in *Sartoris* as well. Crossing it, visitors enter the house through the central hall. The rooms in *Sartoris* are a living room, a lean-to bedroom, and the detached kitchen.

The living room is dominated by the hearth, and it is in this room that the character of the life of the house takes place: "The walls of the room were of chinked logs.... The floor was bare, of hand trimmed boards scuffed with heavy boots and polished by the pads of generations of dogs; two men could lie side by side in the fireplace. In it now four-foot logs blazed against the clay fireback..." (S, p. 309). The epic dimensions of the fireplace give this otherwise Spartan room a majesty befitting the family's head, whose entire mature life—together with the significance of the home he builds to encompass it—is dreamily recollected in the paragraph which follows its description:

> In 1861 he was sixteen and had walked to Lexington, Virginia, and enlisted, served four years in the Stonewall brigade and walked back to Mississippi and built himself a house and got married. His wife's *dot* was a clock and a dressed hog; his own father gave them a mule. His wife was dead these many years, and her successor was dead, but he sat now before the fireplace at which that hog had been cooked, beneath the roof he had built in '66, and on the mantel above him the clock sat, deriding that time whose servant it once had been. (S, p. 310)

The built objects in this description all have a part in concretizing the life lived among them. The roof is a synecdoche for the house which old Virginius built to begin his presencing, his dwelling within it. His family life began with the cooking of the dressed hog on his hearth (not in the kitchen), and the clock on the mantel (though not externally changed) has transformed its station from the service of time to the disarming of it.[8] Whatever scant furniture the MacCallums have, whatever shared life Bayard spends with them, their household is gathered around the three foci archetypically central to any home: the hearth, the dining table, and the bed. Of the week or so of days Bayard visits here, only the first evening is given moment to moment attention, and in this short space of time each of the three foci are engaged in vignettes which depict a simple but right-ordered household to which Bayard has fled and to which his conscience has led him in the hopes of finding some peace. It is important that, for all his previous destructiveness, Bayard behaves quite calmly in the MacCallum house, even while he reproaches himself internally for his cowardice and fear. The simple, quiet, and routine activities of gathering around hearth and table, the orderly business of penning up puppies and possums, and even the passive pursuit of restful sleep are amenities which for a time give Bayard some solace. Waking the second day he hopes for a continuance of the routine: "... he heard a door, and a voice which, with a slight effort of concentration, he knew he could name; and best of all, knew that now he could rise and go where they were gathered about a crackling fire, where light was, and warmth" (p. 324). Bayard's chill is a psychic one, like Narcissa's, assuaged not so much by the warmth of the fire as by the gathering before it.

   Inside and outside are important to Bayard here in terms of the condition of being captured or free. His eagerness to go with Buddy to get the treed possum is part of his affinity and fascination for the bayed and hunted critters he encounters during his stay about the place. His expression as Buddy lifts down the treed possum shows his compassion. With the others in the little possum "jail," it is an animation of his haunted and haggard state. Ellen, the tame fox, is particularly intriguing to Bayard because she is at home and happy, even contented, in the state of being pursued. Bayard is comfortable and at home while he visits the MacCallums, even while he hunts with them. But he must leave before the boys get back from Jefferson with the news of old Bayard's death; and by leaving he becomes an outsider in a number of ways, and in another way the hunted.

Bayard's visits to the MacCallums center more on the hearth and table than the bed. This third focus of the dwelling is, of course, the place for more private communication between family members and friends, and it is here that Buddy MacCallum confides to Bayard his experience in the war and relates how he won a medal. Buddy's bashful pride in his "charm" and his equally modest assessment of army life are opinions he can share at neither hearth nor table, but only in the intimacy of nightfall whisperings.

In "The Tall Men," the bedroom becomes an infirmary and Buddy's bed a focus for gathering the family, which is concerned about his injury. The bleatings of the investigator fail to penetrate the circle of this family turned inward in its concern for its own, and another focus, the kitchen table, is put to use in the service of healing the injury. Just as the MacCallums gather around Buddy's bed while the doctor assesses the damage to his leg, they will soon gather around the table to help amputate the damaged limb. Even in these unusual circumstances, the archetypal foci of the house continue their function of gathering the family.

The yeoman dog-run house is the best place with which to begin consideration of fictive interior elements such as hearth, table, and bed, since it is in this built form that these objects manifest such strong significance. This is not to say that the hearth of a manor house or of a Negro cabin has a less important or different function. In Faulkner's fiction, however, the purest of vernacular meanings for the hearth are those implicit in the dwelling life of the Spartan yeomanry.

Go Down, Moses is a novel which presents a mixed landscape supporting nearly all the various forms of fictive architecture in Yoknapatawpha on all levels, from the natural places of country, region, and landscape to the man-made forms of settlement, communal and domestic building, room, furniture, and meaningful object. Ike McCaslin's cultural and divine history, articulated in his dialog with Cass in section 4 of "The Bear," sets the history of the South as a region within that of the entire country, even the New World versus the Old. The wilderness of the hunting stories is significant specifically on the level of landscape. The settlement—the town of Jefferson—though chiefly in the background, comes to the fore in the concluding title story of the suite. The novel begins at the level of the house with the McCaslin dog-run, the larger

houses of Hubert Beauchamp and old Carothers, the cabins of Lucas
Beauchamp and George Wilkins, and in each their specific meaningful *things:*
doors and windows, desk, table and bed, threshold, and hearth. Beginning on
the early McCaslin farm, the mixed landscape of *Go Down, Moses* leads ever
outward in scope to the broadest meanings of the fictive topos articulated by
the wilderness as a concretization of ontological space.

The McCaslin place, like Sutpen's and others is trying to be a plantation
and almost succeeds by 1837. This is when old Carothers McCaslin dies,
leaving his uncompleted manor house and his disorganized patrimony to his
twin sons, who feel no mandate to complete his house or his dream. The place
is seventeen miles from Jefferson [GDM, pp. 66, 72, 89, 370], in the same area
as the MacCallums. Though there are some inconsistencies in the distances
given to these two farms,[9] it is clear from the stories that MacCallum is a
yeoman hill farm, while the other is a bottomland plantation on which the
McCaslins are trying to live like yeomen. Confusion of the two places is
confounded by their proximity to each other, the slight similarity of names,
and the presence in both houses of a passel of dogs, a tame fox, and a clock on
the mantel.

Buck and Buddy's dog-run cabin is a fine complement to the
MacCallums', notwithstanding the two conflicting tales about its origin.
Section 4 of "The Bear" relates that the twins, "as soon as their father was
buried moved out of the tremendously conceived, the almost barn-like edifice
which he had not even completed, into a one-room log cabin, which the two of
them built themselves and added other rooms to while they lived in it . . . " (p.
262). But the narrative voice of "The Fire and the Hearth" describes the house
as "two log-wings which Carothers McCaslin had built and which had sufficed
old Buck and Buddy, connected by the open hallway which, as his pride's
monument and epitaph, old Cass Edmonds had enclosed and superimposed
with a second storey of white clapboards and faced with a portico" (p. 45).

The first version is to be taken as the more accurate one, since chapter 1 of
"The Fire and the Hearth" is narrated from the often erroneous mind of Lucas
Beauchamp.[10] The more likely version of the history of the house is the one
related in "The Bear," where it begins as a one-room log cabin, with other
rooms added later to make it the four crib dog-trot of "Was," and finally the
complete, enclosed, two-story clapboard and portico enhanced version
which Lucas berates on his approach in "The Fire and the Hearth." Lucas's
belief that old Carothers built the cabin is probably the result of his ancestor-
worship.[11] Had Carothers built a two-room cabin and a large house, the twins
would hardly begin a second log house. In any case, the earliest view of the
McCaslin dog-run—and the first in *Go Down, Moses*—is of its plan,
articulated by the McCaslin dogs running, not up and down the hall, but from
room to room in pursuit of the house fox. It is now 1859, twenty-two years

after the twins built their one-room log cabin. It has been expanded into a four-room house with central hall. The dogs can run from room to room on each side without going out in the hall, indicating doorways between rooms. The dogs are even given their own room.

The first significance of this house comes from its beginnings as a single-crib house. Fundamentally it is a concretization of the McCaslins' humility and independence. They have none of the pretensions or aspirations of their father, and their vision of existence is not only simpler but the better for it.

Secondly, the house is similar in parti with the Beauchamp house, Warwick. In the plan of the dog-run, Buddy's room is the front one. When, on occasion, Hubert must bring Turl back to the McCaslins' himself, he brings his sister, "and they would stay for a week or longer, Miss Sophonsiba living in Uncle Buddy's room and Uncle Buddy moved clean out of the house" (p. 6). Warwick is obviously the standard central hall H-plan house, with kitchen to the rear and bedrooms upstairs. Buck McCaslin's assumption that Sophonsiba's room would likely be at the back of the house is a commonsense conclusion drawn from customary room arrangement. Amodeus assumes Sophonsiba's room is in the rear, "[w]here she can holler down to the kitchen without having to get up," because family bedrooms are usually to the back, with front bedrooms reserved for guests. Not only is the right front (upstairs) bedroom of the Beauchamp house most likely to be the guest room, but it is at the same place in the plan that Sibbey sleeps when a guest at McCaslins'. Knowing the custom at both places, Sibbey is careful to set her trap in the appropriate room.

Though each addition to the growing McCaslin dog-run house is historically noted in various places in *Go Down, Moses*, narrative action takes place only in the four room dog-trot of "Was" and the completed two-story house of "The Fire and the Hearth."

"The Fire and the Hearth" concerns centers, places, domains, and meaningful things. Its level is that of the landscape, though most of the action takes place *on* the earth rather than across the surface of the topos. The significance of other events derives from which rooms they occur in and what objects are involved. Of the various elements then, place, center, and domain are primary; of levels, landscape, room, and object are most important. The Indian mound is the principal place, the hearth is the principal center, and the land Lucas and Roth hunt, farm, and dwell on is their domain. The surface of that domain is a symbolically operative landscape; the commissary and the bedroom are the important rooms; and the significant objects include furniture like the table and the bed or groups of things, such as the machine and the coin and even Nat's cookstove, well, and back porch.

To begin with, "The Fire and the Hearth" is about objects *in* the earth which are meant to stay there (as Molly knows), and about the fever, fire, or

Figure 8-1. Conjectured Plans in "Was"

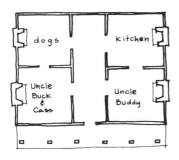

The Mc Caslin Cabin

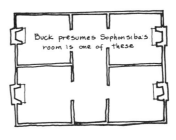

Warwick · Second Floor

desire of acquisitiveness which drives men to try to render out of the earth matter (here, moonshine or buried money) which belongs to it, by the fire of *techne*—that is, machine or still. The story begins with Lucas's attempt to insure his continued success at rendering corn whiskey from the earth by burying his still and exposing George Wilkins's more careless operation. He assures himself of his success with the knowledge that this is his domain: "He had been born on this land, twenty-five years before the Edmonds who now owned it. He had worked on it ever since he got big enough to hold a plow straight; he had hunted over every foot of it during his childhood and youth and his manhood too..." (p. 36). It is also his business territory, from which he renders his product. His knowledge of this domain leads him to a natural place, a natural center to hide his own distilling machinery, "where it would be reasonably safe after the excitement started" (p. 34). While trying to conceal the kettle and tube in the Indian mound, however, Lucas is nearly buried, as the earth itself reclaims the kettle, almost violently, and even paying Lucas for it with the single gold coin. The opening in the mound is the gaping maw of the earth, swallowing the machinery by which Lucas rendered his product. The lesson of this opening event will be spoken only much later by Molly as she expresses to Roth her fears for Lucas's continued attempts to find buried money. "'Because God say, "What's rendered to My earth, it belong to Me unto I resurrect it"...'" (T, p. 102). Lucas misses this point completely, subsumed by a dream of quick riches not unlike that wielded by Flem Snopes on Ratliff, Bookwright, and Armstid in *The Hamlet*, or even that which Lucas himself puts on the salesman. The series of events which follows is the result of Lucas's prideful belief not that he has a right to what he can earn from a crop gotten by scratching the surface of the land he has been given to farm, but that everything within that land is as much his as the crop he can raise on it. The difference between his earlier pursuit of distilling and his later one is that his still was, in a way, like farming: a product was drawn from the earth with work and sweat and transformed into something which could be consumed or sold for money. With the metal detector, Lucas is attempting to draw money directly from the earth. The center of Lucas's life now shifts from his hearth to the Indian mound, as the fire of his avarice subdues the fire on his hearth.

On his walk up to the Edmonds house Lucas notes in particular Roth's tractor shed and garage. He scorns the presence of this machinery, which he believes "Zack Edmonds would not have allowed on the place" (p. 44). Neither would old Cass "have put his foot in" the garage Roth has built for his automobile. But Lucas only appears to judge men by whether they build or not and may not even know that he actually judges *them* rather than what they build. Old Cass, he knows, built a house for Lucas and Molly and lent him the land; and old Carothers, he thinks, built the original dog-trot which Cass later enlarged. What he seems to admire is household founding: building a dwelling and establishing a home within it. He cares little or nothing for additions or architectural appendages such as those wrought by Cass and Roth.

The flashback to Lucas's confrontation with Zack is a rendering of the founding of his own household using the furniture and objects which gather and hold its meaning. Though Cass certainly built the fireplace and hearth with the house, it is Lucas who lights the hearthfire on his wedding day to begin his family's presencing, their active dwelling in the house. The fire provides heat for the house, a focus for gathering, and a symbolization of the living presence within it. The fire on its hearth is a visualization of the *genius loci* of the Beauchamp house.[12] Its uninterrupted continuity is the point; as long as the fire burns, the life of the house continues. Specifically within the story, of course, the fire is the love between Lucas and Molly which animates the *genius loci* of their household. Had Lucas actually doused the fire in his frustration at Molly's long absence it would have signaled a true break with Molly and the loss of love in their household. As it is, her temporary stay in Zack's house dims her presencing in her own home and strains the presence of her love within it.

Beyond its archetypicality, Lucas's hearthfire is local legend in the area around McCaslin. Rider, the widowed sawmill lead man of "Pantaloon in Black," knows the legend in nearly the same words as those with which it is rendered in the earlier story. By now legend has become tradition; and Rider, too, lit his hearthfire on his wedding night (p. 138).

After demanding that Zack send his wife back, Lucas returns to his house among the things of his household, each of which has a personal significance for him. The gate, fence, and path are things that he has made to complement and personalize his place. These things characterize his dwelling as Molly's flower beds do. It is this, her ability to express her love through the unique characterization of their dwelling as their own, which Lucas fears he has lost by her temporary absence. He is in this way another of Faulkner's imperfect or inauthentic dwellers. He has appropriated all things, including the life of his house, to himself; and when part of it is taken away, he feels bereft of part of his being and must confront Zack to reaffirm it.

Because these issues are so deep and personal, the objects and furniture employed at this point in the story are those in private places, like chests of drawers. Lucas's first move is to provide for Molly by leaving her the money from the box under the hearth. The importance of the hearthfire is restated here in the heat from the brick which Lucas removes; "a slow, deep solidity of heat, a condensation of the two years during which the fire had burned constantly above it, a condensation not of fire but of time" (p. 51). The reminder here is that the fire, not the hearth alone, is the *animus*; the warmth of the household is generated *into* the hearth. From beneath this firebrick Lucas draws his treasure. Though it may be said that he is again rendering from the earth, this money is certainly his, as this piece of earth is, a place he has made his own by founding his hearthfire here. But the box which holds his treasure does have a parallel meaning to his house. All these containers for his treasures have been given him by McCaslins: the house by Cass, the dispatch box from old Carothers, and the walnut chest of draws from Isaac. From this last more intimate piece of furniture, Lucas draws the razor with which he will confront Zack.

It is not by mere circumstance that this confrontation takes place over Zack's bed. Lucas seeks Zack in his bedroom because it is the place where the transgression would have happened. The bed—or, rather, its use—is the thing in question. And as Lucas keeps the razor in his bureau, Zack keeps his pistol in his drawer, not in his bed. Zack's response to Lucas's demand to reach under his pillow for his pistol is a reprimand: "It's not under the pillow. It's in that drawer yonder where it always is and you know it..." (p. 53). The implication is clear: a man who would keep a pistol in his bed might keep other inappropriate things there too, perhaps another man's wife. Zack knows that Lucas challenges only a supposed transgression, that Lucas does not really believe that Zack would lie down with Molly. So Zack voices the fact that Lucas knows his integrity by affirming that he keeps his pistol where it ought to be. Since Lucas forces the issue, Zack arranges the room for confrontation. He places the bed between them, closes and locks the door to make the room a completely intimate enclosure, and puts the pistol where Lucas hinted it ought to be for the kind of man Lucas is suggesting he is. Despite the fact that Lucas wins the struggle, the misfired cartridge verifies the truth of Zack's honorable conduct.

Lucas's informing on George's whiskey operation is another form of his territoriality. Forty-five years after founding his own household, he is trying to prevent George from starting a family with his daughter, not so much because of George's brash and foolish ways, but because he is "an interloper without forbears and sprung from nowhere and whose very name was unknown in the country twenty-five years ago" (p. 40). With Nat's help though, George is clever enough to get Lucas entangled in his arrest. Under these circumstances, the young couple not only gains Lucas's permission to marry (after the fact), but is able to extort from Lucas the basic needs of their own house.

None of Nat's requirements for a household are traditional. They are the basic needs of a utilitarian homemaker, without burden of significance: a back porch that works,[13] a cook stove for food (not a hearth), and a well for water. Even when George mentions that his hearth ("chimbly") is suitable for cooking, Lucas's daughter reemphasizes her preference for a cook stove. Hers is another, leaner generation who care nothing for hearths or hearthfires.

With his daughter's house set in order and George running his kettle, Lucas can now return to his concern with the Indian mound. The remainder of the story depicts Lucas's single-minded pursuit of buried money and its near-destruction of the household Lucas has fought so hard to maintain. Molly's appeal for a "vo'ce" from Lucas stirs in Roth two images at polar opposites in the spectrum of fictive architecture—a geographic conception of how far Lucas's family has dispersed, and another recollection, again with furniture, of Roth's own earlier years with Henry.

In response to Molly's petition, Roth recalls that Lucas's sister Fonsiba "married and went to Arkansas to live.... But James, the eldest, ran away before he became of age and didn't stop until he had crossed the Ohio River.... It was as though he had not only (as his sister was later to do) put running water between himself and the land of his grandmother's betrayal and his father's nameless birth, but he had interposed latitude and geography too ..." (p. 105). Faulkner here leaves the spheres of landscape, topography, and even region to graph the diaspora of the Beauchamps. Latitude and geography are global dimensions for distance. Tennie's Jim first uses running water, a topographical item, to separate himself from his family and his blood, then seems to leap clear even of state boundaries. Roth recalls the scattering here because Lucas and Molly are the last members of their family to remain, and now Molly, the source of this cohesion, wants to go too.

Thoughts of the unity of the Beauchamp family stir in Roth images of his own part of that cohesion, of his foster brother Henry, and of his own separation from their household. Again the rendering is in terms of furniture and things, and as Zack and Lucas faced each other over the bed, Roth and Henry confront age-old differences in an argument over who will sleep where. Until he was seven, Roth was as much a member of the Beauchamp household as of his own. There is a pallet bed and a dining table in both houses and probably another hearth in Roth's, (though it is not mentioned here), and

Roth recalls that even "before he was out of infancy, the two houses had become interchangeable: himself and his foster brother sleeping on the same pallet in the white man's house or in the same bed in the negro's and eating of the same food at the same table in either, actually preferring the negro house, the hearth on which even in summer a little fire always burned, centering the life in it, to his own" (p. 110). Again the life of both houses here is depicted in terms of three foci; and aside from the explicit rendering of the hearth's significance, it is important to note that Roth and Henry share neither the bed at Roth's house nor the pallet at Henry's. For Roth to come down to Henry's pallet in Zack's house is as much a courtesy as the respect which Henry shows Roth in his own home. When the segregatory incident comes, the sharing of the other two foci is also abrogated: Roth is prepared a separate place at table as well, and henceforth shares neither hearth nor hunt.

With these profound memories in mind, Roth goes to Lucas's house to dissuade him from divorce. In his frustration with Zack, Lucas nearly doused his own hearthfire. Now in the depths of stubbornness and facing the impending breakup of his household, the contemptuous Lucas spits into his own hearth. The nature of Lucas's emotional state causes in each case an inverse reaction. A hearthfire is a thing neither so intense as to need a bucket of water to drown, nor so niggardly that spitting could subdue it. As frustration generates overreaction and contempt produces a minimal response, each of these gestures is appropriately opposite. Lucas's spitting into his hearth is the nadir of the story and the indication of his utter contempt for the elementals of hearth, stone, and fire which were once so meaningful to him. It is a gesture in favor of the mechanicals of metal detector and coin which now animate or give purpose to his existence. Even when compared to Nat and George's dream of utilitarian existence, Lucas seems to be the one who has repudiated his hearth—a useful amenity—in favor of a machine he feels is a necessity but which really is not. Lucas finally sees his error when the earth itself nearly claims Molly. After his divorce is struck from the docket, Lucas comes to surrender the divining machine to Roth. He comes while Roth is eating dinner and sets it on the opposite end of the dining table. Cleaned of mud and stripped of its function, it now becomes a significant object, nearly possessing the familiarity of a common household thing. Roth proposes to keep it in the place where other memorabilia are kept—the attic. Though Lucas has never had an attic, he understands the kind of room it is and that Roth is asking if he might need the machine again someday. "In the attic" means more than "here"; it is "here and protected, here and remembered, here and treasured for its long and meaningful past." Lucas's answer carries the finality of his decision. He tells Roth to "get rid of it . . . clean off this place" (p. 130), by which he means a great deal more than "away." By "off this place" Lucas means not only to send the machine away but to commit it to oblivion—

send it out of memory, unprotected and utterly gone. The detector is not even useful as a reminder, since his own hearth is the positive signifier for the home which the machine nearly destroyed.

Hearth and fire are strangely absent from mention in either Roth's or Zack's dwellings. Though beneath its second-story clapboard and behind its portico is the original McCaslin dog-run (with one hearth, certainly, for each room), the only fire mentioned is that which Lucas tends in the kitchen stove while Molly delivers the infant Roth. The absence of such hearthfire may indicate a lack of love in Roth's upbringing and a possible cause for his behavior in "Delta Autumn."

The two true mansions in *Go Down, Moses* are old Carothers's ("the concrete indication of his own vanity's boundless conceiving") which becomes a home in spite of itself, a dwelling, and Warwick, the Beauchamp place, which (in contrast to the McCaslin house) suffers the same fate—and from similar causes—as Sutpen's mansion.

Like the early Sutpen house, Carothers McCaslin's half-built one is missing many of its windows "and had no back door at all" (p. 262). The reason is the same: only when it becomes a dwelling will it acquire the details of vital existence. As an incomplete structure, the house is only an enclosure for the gentlemen's agreement which the twins have with their slaves, with a *de jure* opening at the front door and a *de facto* one in back.[14] Later, completed by Buck and Sophonsiba, it becomes a real dwelling: "They moved back into the big house, the tremendous cavern which old Carothers had started and never finished, cleared the remaining negroes out of it and with his mother's dowry completed it, at least the rest of the windows and doors and moved into it, all of them save Uncle Buddy who declined to leave the cabin he and his twin had built..." (p. 301).

The external significance of this house is found in its off-stage or otherwise less apparent details. First, Isaac McCaslin is born in this house, the completed McCaslin mansion. This is the one he is to inherit, and he is expected to found his own home within it. This is the house his wife hopes to move into when she queries Ike about his farm. Second, Buck and Sophonsiba lead a blameless existence here. Their decade of family life reveals none of the vices which haunted the rest of the McCaslin line and threatened any who would complete the embodiment of old Carothers's dream. But for Isaac, orphaned at nine, the mansion is not really home because he is not nurtured there. Though his cousin McCaslin is "rather his brother than cousin and rather his father than either" (p. 4), his true foster father is, of course, Sam Fathers. It is because the site of Ike's primary nurturing shifts from the home to the wilderness that he has no special attachment for his family house. With Ike's coming of age, Cass now moves back to the twins' old dog-run, leaving the mansion for Ike to live in. When Ike rents a room in Jefferson instead,

Cass cannot understand ("Why should I sleep here in my house when you wont sleep yonder in yours?"). As Ike cannot accept the land without denying the values he has learned in the wilderness, he cannot dwell in the old home because it is not the place in which he was nurtured in those values. Despite the fact that Ike later finds his room "wall-less and topless and floorless in glory" (pp. 311–12) in the early days of his marriage, it may be said that he never truly dwells in any house again. Cass continues to live in the twins' dog-trot, which he will later expand to the two-story house of "The Fire and the Hearth." Old Carothers's house stands empty. Because McCaslin cannot live in it and Isaac will not, it will never be lived in again.

The power (and the grace) which Sophonsiba has for making homes is evident in the ease with which she convinces Buck to finish old Carothers's house and move into it. Though she appears a bit silly in "Was" with her trace chains jewelry, fluttering handkerchief, and insistence on calling the place Warwick, her idealism maintains the standards of the place as long as she lives there. When she wins and marries Theophilus, the same idealism is carried to old Carothers's house, and it is this spirit which animates its completion. The McCaslin house becomes a family dwelling when Sibbey causes it to have windows and doors.

Though men are the home builders and founders here, women are home makers and keepers. Hubert's father built the Beauchamp house, or so the narration says, but in discovering Hubert's transgression, Sophonsiba laments, "My mother's house! Defiled!" (p. 303). The McCaslin mansion is completed with Sophonsiba's dowry, and the lot and building materials for the bungalow Ike builds for his wife are from her dowry. These details, together with the fact that Faulkner's dog-runs are mostly bachelor habitations, supports the conjecture that McCaslin expanded the twins' dog-run when he married his wife Alice (though he may have begun any time after the death of the twins, when he assumed management of the farm). In any case he has no interest in either beginning or continuing life in old Carothers's house.

The internal significance of the McCaslin mansion lies again in a particular piece of furniture. Though its hearths and beds are hardly mentioned, its dining room table is the focus for Hubert's endowment to Isaac of fifty gold pieces and the silver cup: "two weeks after his birth in 1867, the first time he and his mother came down stairs, one night and the silver cup sitting on the cleared dining-room table beneath the bright lamp . . . " (p. 301). The entire family, including Tennie, are gathered to witness this legacy. When Ike reaches twenty-one, though all but Cass have died, it is "this same table in this same room by the light even of this same lamp" (p. 307) where he and Cass discover the remainder of his legacy: Hubert's IOUs in the tin coffee pot. The significance of the table and the lamp is not that family matters are being brought before them to be dealt with, but that the table and lamp are the same ones as before, and that all other things *should* have been as before. The dining table is the place where things are promised, given, and dispensed. The fact that all other things are still here and unchanged emphasizes the transubstantiation of the legacy into something completely different from what it was when last it rested on the table. The place and its meaning are the same, only the substance of the legacy has changed.

Meanwhile, without Sibbey's presence, Warwick and its earl go downhill together. Even while Sophonsiba lives there, the place seems to be barely holding its own. The gateposts are without gates, and there are a broken shutter and a rotted floorboard in the back gallery. Yet repairs for such things as these are Hubert's business, and Sibbey does the best she can in maintaining her garden.

The deteriorating Warwick reappears late in section 4 of "The Bear": "the shabby and overgrown entrance . . . the paintless house which . . . on the inside seemed each time larger because . . . there was less and less in it of the fine furnishings . . ." (p. 302). Though Sibbey's discovery of Hubert's turpitude is only a glimpsed memory for Ike, the scene which she causes in the "barren unswept hall" is long and animated enough to give adequate reason for Warwick's Sutpen-like spontaneous combustion. In addition, the gradual but steady disappearance of furniture from the place, aided by Sibbey's own filching, is symptomatic of the growing poverty which explains (though it does not excuse) Hubert's periodic pilfering from his godson's legacy. Ike's last recollection of the house is a vision of his uncle standing before a dark and decaying hearth: "the cold unswept hearth in which the very bricks themselves were crumbling into a litter of soot and dust and mortar and the droppings of chimney-sweeps" (p. 304). Though the family has gathered here before the hearth, Hubert has gathered them to witness his continuing lie, the lie in his locked closet, of his godson's diminishing bequest.

Taking what is left of his eroded inheritance and relinquishing the McCaslin farm, Isaac goes into Jefferson to live in a rented room. From here to the boarding house where he lives with his wife, and on to the house he builds for her, in one room of which he still lives in his old age, the question remains: where does Ike McCaslin dwell? The answer is, of course, in the wilderness, and it is evident not only in his loving view of it but in the nature of the wilderness itself.

Ike's habitation of the built environment is at best tenuous, for he seems to be camping where others dwell, dwelling where visiting hunters only camp. At first he lives "in one small cramped fireless rented room in a Jefferson boarding house" (p. 300). The room is specifically fireless and the house a lodging for temporary existence, a shelter for men of no place. His address for the greater part of his life is the single room of his dead wife's house. His few possessions are "his kit of brand new carpenter's tools...the shotgun McCaslin had given him...General Compson's compass (and...horn too) and the iron cot and mattress and the blankets which he would take each fall into the woods for more than sixty years and the bright tin coffee pot" (p. 300). This is a catalog of the things only suggested in the opening of the novel as belonging to a man "who in all his life had owned but one object more than he could carry in his pockets and his hands at one time" (p. 3). Most of these things have to do with his life in the woods, but only one of them—his cot—is an archetypal object of dwelling. Though he surely has a bed in his room in the Jefferson bungalow, it is never mentioned. And though he spends far more time here than in the woods, his use of the cot is rendered only in "Delta Autumn," leaving no doubt as to his true dwelling place.

As Ike lies quietly in the pitched tent, his perceptions are evidence that only bare essentials are necessary to dwell. There is no hearth here, but only "a good fire in the sheet-iron heater" (p. 349), no four-poster bed, only "the strong, battered iron cot, [and] the stained mattress" (p. 349). His recollection of the six room house at De Spain's hunting camp reminds him that its "roof...had become his home" (p. 351). But it is the meaning of the space which precipitates the act of dwelling, not the architectural solidification of it, so that even though "for almost fifty years now the house had not even existed, the conviction, the sense and feeling of home, had been merely transferred into the canvas...because even this tent with its muddy floor and the bed...was his home" (pp. 351-52).

Among these thoughts, too, are Ike's recollections of his house in Jefferson and of its building. Though all efforts of house-building have to do with home-founding, Ike's home was forever lost to him when his wife became "lost." Though he continues to live in the house without family, he never thinks of it as home. His true home is the place where he lives with "his mistress and his wife," the woods; his dwelling place is the wilderness.

"The Woods...His Mistress and His Wife"

The area of Faulkner's Yoknapatawpha called the Big Bottom is fictive natural place, the concretization of sacred space in a sacred landscape. The wilderness stories disclose the gradual deterioration of a cultural vision which continued to show piety as a natural response to a wilderness still considered sacred. [15] The big woods is Faulkner's most expressive natural place and an arena for the practice of reverence towards the spiritual incarnate in the natural.

The cartography of the sacred wilderness on the Yoknapatawpha map can be seen as a reversal of the archetype illustrated by Yi-Fu Tuan in *Topophilia*. Early views of the New World wilderness correspond to this

Figure 8-2. Tuan's Topology and Faulkner's Topos

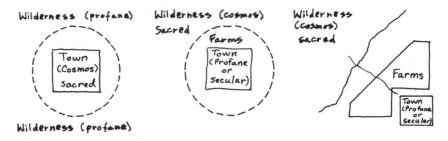

archetype because the dense forests and rich undergrowth of the interior gave early settlers no referent to Biblical descriptions of a desolate and accursed wasteland, or the desert of temptation and banishment. The wilderness, then, became the dark woods of temptation and banishment, the haunt of demons and evil spirits, and the wilderness and the town were counterposed as profane and sacred, respectively.[16] In Faulkner the conditions are reversed: the town is profane and the wilderness is sacred space. Though Yoknapatawpha's wilderness does not surround the tamed land except when Jefferson is still the settlement of Habersham, the linear path to the edges of the wilderness still leads out from a profane center to a sacred wood which stretches away indefinitely in at least two directions—north across the Tallahatchie River and southwest to the Delta.

On the whole critical interpretation of Faulkner's wilderness and its theology has tended to see it as a product of the legacy given him from the supposedly continuous literary tradition of doctrinaire transcendentalist and Pantheist thinking from within the work of Emerson, Whitman, and Thoreau to Hawthorne and Melville.[17] Though certain of Leo Marx's references to the Edenic and pastoral archetype later invaded by the steam engine recall the serene aura of Yoknapatawpha's Big Bottom, Faulkner's wilderness is neither Biblical wilderness nor Biblical garden. The big woods is very much a dark paradise, the garden after the Fall. It is formidable country, inhabited also by visible and invisible presences whose referents are the natural spirits of Indian legend rather than the ubiquitous godhead of Walden Pond. The spirit incarnate in the buck which Sam salutes as "Grandfather" is not only his own ancestor, but the Father of Grandfathers and one of the nature spirits of pre-Classical history, preexistent to the gods of mythology. To the native American these spirits are incarnate in the oak and the pine, the swamp and the waterfall, as well as in the deer and the bear.[18]

Yet this is a wilderness where the "ancient immortal Umpire" is without doubt an omnipotent and benevolent divinity, and the magnanimity of the Natural Law's administrator is revealed in its being "not quite inimical because they were too small" (p. 177),[19] where the loving generosity of the Creator is seen in the lush abundance of a nearly impenetrable plant growth and a plenitude of animal life spirited enough to be animated illustrations of the virtues needed to live in the profane world, in uncomplicated lessons which the young can understand.

The primary emotions of this, Faulkner's finest natural place, are the submissive respect for nature held by the Southerner and described by Donald Davidson, and a piety for the created world as a dwelling place for all communicative spirits. The wilderness is more than just the land which the Chickasaw once thought was his, or the collection of creatures which live within it. It is a meaningful place of its own.

To say that natural or man-made place embodies meanings is to say that its details, its characteristics, express its significance. The big woods of the hunting stories has certain very definite topological characteristics, perceivable in three separate conditions.

It is first a space with somewhat immeasurable dimensions. The wilderness has a mythical *scale* which radically effects one's sense of progression or movement: "dwarfed by that perspective into an almost ridiculous diminishment, the surrey itself seemed to have ceased to move" (p. 195).[20] It has but one boundary, where "the skeleton stalks of cotton and corn in the last of the open country" run up against "the tall and endless wall of dense November woods" (p. 195). This wall is entered through an opening as one would enter through a door, so that the wall is a kind of "architectural event,"[21] the door a threshold into a different existential space. Once the *boundary* is crossed, once the space is entered, the opening disappears, and there is no longer an outside. The wilderness in effect becomes a place unto itself, almost a state of being, an aura with a sensibly different atmosphere. The *density* of the landscape, the topological attribute by which the path opens before the wagon and closes behind it,[22] contributes to this sense of enclosure, of almost an immersion within the space.

The element which is most responsible for the content, scale, and density of the wilderness is its timber. "The Old People" distinguishes the components of the big woods as oak, cypress, and gum trees, a nearly impenetrable undergrowth of cane and briar, and a spirit, an immortal Umpire which watches from *beyond* and above the trees (pp. 176–77). The height of this timber lends veneration and the sense of longevity (even permanence, not to say a name) to the Big Woods. Four of the six principal scenes in the wilderness stories are at specified trees. Ike's vision of the buck which Sam salutes takes place where "he and Sam stood motionless against a tremendous pin oak in a little thicket" (p. 181). A year earlier, as Ike stood with Sam "against a big gum tree beside a little bayou" (p. 202), Old Ben comes to look him over without being seen himself. And when Ike rescues the fyce from Old

Figure 8-3. Mississippi and Yazoo Delta Forest Types

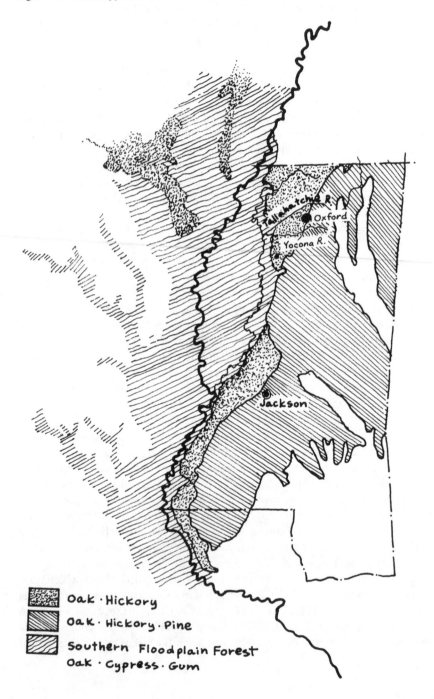

Oak · Hickory

Oak · Hickory · Pine

Southern Floodplain Forest
Oak · Cypress · Gum

Ben, the bear has "turned at bay against the trunk of a big cypress" (p. 211). By themselves these specifics are of little importance, though the associative attributes of the trees contribute to the scene. In the sequence of events the gum tree appears first, then the oak near which Ike sees the buck, then the cypress tree. The gum is the most plebian of the three, which may add significance to the well-known gum tree scene with Boon and the squirrels. But the permanence of oak adds to the sense of the immortality of the place and of the buck here, just as the majesty and incorruptibility of cypress are qualities attributed to Old Ben. Though the gum tree beloved of the squirrels may or may not speak of the commonality of Boon's temper, the scene does not take place *in* the woods but "just outside" it, so that his actions are not really a profanation of the sacred wood. And in the most important of the tree scenes—Ike's first vision of the Old Ben—the tree is unspecified. It is more a vertical marker, the center of the figure of infinity (∞) which Old Ben leads Ike to trace on the ground, bringing him back to the same sacred space in which he surrendered his worldly objects to witness the bear's theophany.

Space in both stories is rendered in terms of the time it takes to move within it: "Sam led them for an hour through the grey and unmarked afternoon.... Sam led them on foot now, unpathed through the markless afternoon ... the dizzy rushing of time in which the buck ... was moving (pp. 179–80).... as though time were merely something he walked through as he did through air ... " (p. 228). Hunters and game seem to move in an enclosure of time, and in both "The Old People" and "The Bear" the world outside the big woods does not exist for the hunters until such *time* as they leave camp. Being in the wilderness also has its own particular kind of time, as spoken by Uncle Ash when Ike holds up his watch near the closing scene of "The Bear": "That's town time. You aint in town now. You in the woods" (p. 323). The wilderness is thus an ontological condition with meaningful time as its measure.[23] This understanding is merely the obverse side of Faulkner's use of space/time in the "time and its furniture" metaphor of *Sartoris/Flags in the Dust*: Time is like a room, an enclosure of space, dwelling in which teaches the ends of wisdom. In "The Bear" the long series of events which is the legend of Old Ben is rendered as a space, "a corridor of wreckage and destruction beginning back before the boy was born ... " (p. 193). Time, then, is like an enclosed space, and certain spaces, such as the wilderness, are rendered in time.

Lastly, the wilderness is a person, with a sensible presence. It has the consciousness of a person, perceptible in certain descriptive passages in "The Old People":

"profound, sentient, gigantic and brooding..." (p. 175)

"[it] seemed to lean, stooping a little, watching them and listening... brooding, secret, tremendous, almost inattentive..." (p. 177) "the slow and shifting yet constant walls from beyond and above which the wilderness watched them pass..." (p. 178)

"the wilderness breathed again. It seemed to lean inward above them...tremendous, attentive, impartial and omniscient..." (p. 181)

"tremendous and impartial and waiting" (p. 182)

This sentient spirit inhabits the body of the wilderness, the big woods, and except for one of two passages which refer to Ike and the wilderness as two persons (pp. 354 and 326), it is found exclusively in "The Old People" section of the novel. In "The Bear" the wilderness is primarily a sacred space perceived as an aura.

The wilderness is certainly home for the creatures who live within it, most notably the buck and Old Ben. The domesticated animals have a more difficult time, depending on the degree of their domestication. Like the surrey, the mule which bolts at the scent of Old Ben belongs to civilization and not to the woods. Those who have been touched by the wilderness, however, like the old bitch that "had to be brave once so she could keep on calling herself a dog" and the maimed mule which would stand, are more at home there. But the wilderness only smites temerity, and visitors to the wilderness with the proper quality of fear and piety are accepted.

Few *men* can be said to truly dwell in the big woods. The Chickasaws, of course, were its first human inhabitants. However, after their departure west there seems to be only Jobaker left, and when he dies there is a definite mysticism with which Sam Fathers assumes his place. A broad view of the three hunting stories suggests that the *genius loci* of the wilderness requires an attendant spirit, not to see to its needs as a place, which as the "ancient immortal umpire" it can surely do, but as an objectification of itself, an Other to or with which it can "speak," commiserate, even love. The attendant of the wilderness thus becomes another Adam, not in the sense of a new man, but as a being in the body of the world with whom the spirit can communicate. The assumption here is that the *genius loci* of the wilderness has the capacity for love. And the knowledge which Jobaker holds innately and which Sam Fathers knows from his blood is the knowledge which Sam must *teach* Ike, because he is not of the blood. He teaches Ike the values and love of the wilderness with the blood of the wilderness itself—that of the buck—and *charges* him with it. From innate knowledge to blood knowledge to education, the wisdom to be passed on is slipping further and further from its source. The question which remains is the same old one: Will Roth's son be able to learn the same wisdom, given in love by the *genius loci* of the wilderness now past, from a hunting horn given him as an infant by a seventy-year-old man?

In any case, there is no doubt that Sam is attached to the land, the wilderness. He belongs to it; it is his home, his domain, and he enters it as anyone would enter his dwelling, through its door: "The boy would watch him for a while against that tall and secret wall, growing smaller and smaller against it, never looking back. Then he would enter it, returning to what the boy believed, and thought that his cousin McCaslin believed, was his loneliness and solitude" (p. 177). It is clear from this passage that the old Indian is not alone in the woods, even after the hunters have all left. Sam Fathers *dwells* in the wilderness and is "the mouthpiece of the host" (p. 171). When he dies, the blood and the knowledge are separate, in Boon and in Ike, so that Boon must perform the burial, but Ike must attend.

"The Old People" generates two other significant features: an architectural relationship of conveyances and a postural relationship of place. There are designated and strictly assigned appropriate places for each of the conveyances in the story. Though the hunters leave town with horses, a wagon, and a surrey in which the older men ride—"the old men in whom the blood ran cold and slow" (p. 179)—only the mounts and the wagon are brought into the woods. The more sophisticated carriage, the vehicle and equipage of the civilized and refined world, is out of place in the wilderness and belongs on the road with the houses, barns, and fences. At one point, on the last great hunting trip when Old Ben is killed, the surrey is kept in a local farmer's stable (p. 251). Only the pioneer conveyance is allowed into the woods.

Throughout both "The Old People" and "The Bear" are several relationships such as this—planar relationships of vertical hierarchy and of horizontal orientation, most of which are articulated by the figure of a man or men on the landscape. In *Go Down, Moses*, in general, the wilderness is vertical and the land horizontal. When part 4 of "The Bear" begins with the statement that Ike and Cass are juxtaposed "not against the wilderness but against the land" (p. 255), the phrase means something more than the movement from the hunting values to the values of civilization. The wilderness is the arena where vertical relationships are exercised, while the tamed land is the place where horizontal relationships prevail. The hierarchical relationship to the topography suggested in the "Vendée" section of *The Unvanquished* is only partially maintained in "The Bear": hunters dismount for the more elemental business of the kill or simply stand and wait for the game to be run by them. The idea of stance, posture, is delineated in an early tableau from Ike's memory:

> Each morning Sam would take the boy out to the stand allotted him. It would be one of the poorer stands of course, since he was only ten and eleven and twelve and he had never even seen a deer running yet. But they would stand there, Sam a little behind him and without a gun himself, as he had been standing when the boy shot the running rabbit when he was eight years old. They would stand there in the November dawns, and after a while they would hear the dogs. (p. 176)

The place (and it is very much a *place*) where the hunter waits is called a stand for obvious reasons, but there is a larger meaning implicit in the passage. For one thing, as Norberg-Schulz notes, "man's active relationship to the world is characterized by his vertical position; he takes 'a stand.' "[24] To stand is to have posture, an attitude and bearing, and a few pages earlier we have been told that Sam "bore himself... with gravity and dignity..." (p. 170). Sam now stands behind the boy as his mentor, and after Ike becomes a man, Sam stands *beside* him to salute the spirit of the wild in the figure of the great buck. Sitting usually indicates a baser task than one's station deserves, as when Boon is described as "never [having] killed anything larger than a squirrel and that sitting..." (p. 176). He is also found sitting, of course, in the gum tree scene.

Sitting as a posture may also indicate the lower end of one's given station, as when Sam is seen sitting in the door of the blacksmith shop where he did carpenter work. But standing is the proper stance for hunting; and though Sam and Ike may be "sitting beneath the close fierce stars on a summer hilltop while they waited for the hounds to bring the fox back within hearing" (p. 170), they are both "standing when the boy [shoots] the running rabbit" (p. 176).

The postural complements to the sitting/standing relationship of man to the horizontal plane of the landscape are the vertical relationships of proximity/distance and orientation. The proximity or distance of one thing to another depends on their proper places. The density of the wilderness renders the proximate/distant relationship as a simple visible/invisible condition. In Ike's first encounter with Old Ben, the bear ranges just outside his and Sam's view. The following summer, Ben lets himself be seen by appearing just at the edge of their field of vision, between foreground and background. Finally, familiar, almost friends, Ike and the bear are in immediate proximity when he rescues the fyce.

Orientation in "The Bear" presents three of the most significant images on the plane of the landscape. Cardinal points are less important here than things like the direction of entry into the wilderness from a clearing without.

The postural orientations of Sam, Boon, Old Ben, and even Lion in the most dramatic scenes are particularly significant as meaningful figures on the landscape. As the bear surges up in the grip of Lion's jaws, both Boon and Lion are free of the earth; and though Ben can lift them both, he must stand on his hind legs like a man, and himself half-free of earth to do so. In the proximity of death, Old Ben turns and, "still carrying the man and the dog," he takes "two or three steps toward the woods on its hind feet as a man would have walked and crashed down" (p. 241). This turning is nothing less than a fundamental and instinctual orientation towards (and a return to) the wilderness as the source, the body of the world. The bear stands and turns to face the woods before he dies. It is to the same purpose that the hunters carry the dying Lion "out to the gallery and put him down facing the woods" (p. 247), where "from time to time the great blue dog would open his eyes, not as if he were listening to them but as though to look at the woods for a moment before closing his eyes again, to remember the woods or to see that they were still there" (p. 248). And as Sam lies in his hut dying (though only Ike knows), the boy imagines that "Sam's eyes were probably open again on that profound look which saw further than them or the hut, further than the death of a bear and the dying of a dog" (p. 245).

A catalog of the big woods distinguishes it as a landscape with three particular areas: the domain of the hunters, Old Ben's domain, and the area of the bear's legend, all of which overlap.[25] The first is given by the range of Ike's wanderings as an experienced woodsman. The rotted log where he and Sam find Old Ben's print is three hours away by mule through dense woods, or about six miles from camp (p. 200). It is "a section of country he had never seen before" (p. 200), and presumably neither have the other hunters. The following summer, when Ike sees the bear, he is nine hours from camp, on foot, half again as far as Sam had led him. Jason Compson's remarks six years later confirm this distance as ten miles (pp. 250–51). Ike's range and domain are larger than those of the other hunters. Their domain seems to be, then, an area of only five miles in any direction from the camp. Where it overlaps Old Ben's territory is where they encounter him. The problem—and the question—is the extent of the old bear's domain.

The hunting stories hold the curiosity that although the map places the camp near the bank of the Tallahatchie, the hunters seldom cross the river to hunt. When they do, it is because Ben has fled across it. Twice the bear takes to the river to lose Boon and Lion, and twice they track him on the other (north) bank before dark overtakes them (pp. 224–25). It is clear from these trackings, and above all from the scene of Old Ben's death, that the river is an edge, a threshold to his exclusive domain.[26] Here he feels safe, while on the hunting camp side he must risk himself before the guns and dogs.

The extent of Old Ben's legend is an intermediate area between these two domains, with rather indistinct boundaries. It is specifically noted as "an area almost a hundred miles square" (p. 193) and so could be either the complete northwest quadrant of the Yoknapatawpha map or an area roughly five miles in any direction from the location of the camp on the Tallahatchie River. The latter possibility may be dismissed for two reasons. First, half of this area is the wilderness directly across the river from camp, and the bear cannot be said to have "earned for himself a name" in uninhabited wilderness. Second, since the legend is of corn-cribs, grown pigs, and calves (as well as traps, deadfalls, and mangled dogs), the area of the legend must partially involve the corn and cotton farms at the edges of the wilderness.

Figure 8-4. Old Ben's Domain

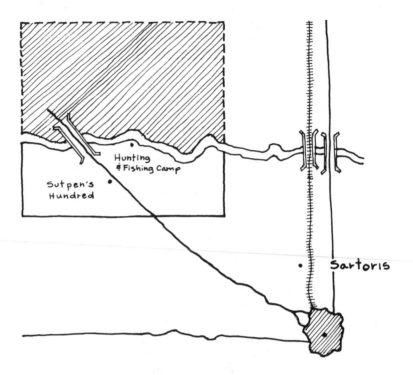

So the domains of Old Ben and the hunters are separated by the river and the area of Ben's legend is where he encroaches on inhabited territory. This leaves only the residual question of which direction Ike travels when he goes ten miles to see the bear for the first time. Faulkner would almost certainly mention the river if Ike had crossed it. And with roads and farms to the west, south, and east, there are few directions left for a ten-mile trek. Since Ike is, at this point, said to be "farther into the new and alien country than he had ever been" (p. 207), and since he crosses neither the river nor Sutpen's vast fields to the south and southwest of the camp,[27] it can only be conjectured that Ike heads west along the river bottoms, crosses the northwest road, then either continues west or heads southwest, probably off the Yoknapatawpha map. Southwest is also the direction of the Yazoo Delta and the retreating wilderness of "Delta Autumn." Though—because of the mythical tenor of the earlier stories—the direction of travel is not crucial, it remains somewhat of a question.

Ike's complete surrender to the wilderness before seeing the bear is important to the relationship of orientation and dwelling. The nature of the condition of being lost centers on disorientation. A person is lost when he can find no bearings with which he is familiar.[28] The opposite of the fearful condition of being lost is the peaceful condition of *belonging*, composed of a knowledge of one's surroundings, or orientation, and a feeling of being at peace in a protected enclosure.[29] As Ike stands "alien and lost in the green and soaring gloom of the markless wilderness" (p. 208), he knows he is "still tainted." At last surrendering the watch and compass, he becomes *utterly* lost, though he is presumably no longer alien since he has now "relinquished completely to it." Through his double back-track, tracing the figure of infinity on the earth, Ike is led back to his point of origin by the old bear himself, so that his vision of the bear comes at the precise place where his belonging began—at the bush where he hung the compass and watch. The paradox of Ike's condition is that it is only when he becomes disoriented and unprotected that he *dwells* most completely in the wilderness and is open to the vision of Old Ben. Topologically lost, he is ontologically at home.

The big woods contains, of course, few built forms. The hunting camp is composed of "the clearing, the house, the barn and its tiny lot with which Major de Spain in his turn had scratched punily and evanescently at the wilderness" (p. 206). The house is described earlier as "a paintless six-room bungalow set on piles above the spring high water" (p. 196). Other than these structures there is only Sam's hut, and the corn crib which he uses to train Lion. The mention of Cassius de Spain, however, affirms a contention noted above in chapter 4: that the hunting and fishing camp of *Go Down, Moses* is not the same as that of Sutpen's Hundred in *Absalom, Absalom!*, though both share a common fictive history. The land is bought by Sutpen in 1833. The fishing camp, built in 1838, is already "abandoned and rotting" when Wash Jones lives there in 1860. He is living there still, with his daughter, when he kills Sutpen in 1869. In the chronology of *Go Down, Moses*, De Spain acquires the land from Sutpen in 1865, restores the camp and begins hunting parties long before 1869. The descriptive passage in "The Bear" suggests that De Spain was the builder of this camp and associates him with the others who scratch and gnaw at the edge of the wilderness with plows and axes (pp. 193, 195, et passim).[30]

The other difference between the two camps is exegetical: Sutpen's camp is a place of unnatural hunt and unholy death, but De Spain's is a center from which the hunters begin the annual celebration and "pageant-rite of the old bear's furious immortality" (p. 194). When it does become a place of dying, it is a ritual of some sacredness for the participants. The sacramental nature of Ike's visit to the burial place of Old Ben and Sam Fathers in his last visit to the area is an indication of the sacred character of this place, as the four corner-markers are indications of its sacred character as a cemetery. And it is some distance away from this knoll that Ike encounters the snake.

The wilderness of the Delta is the largest single expanse of fictive landscape in the Yoknapatawpha canon, only because the boundaries of the Big Bottom of the Tallahatchie are less distinct. As examples of fictive architecture at the landscape level, these two areas complete the range of Faulkner's imagined places, from the compact examples of single houses and their interior spaces to larger clusters of structures and spaces.

9

Fictive Cosmography

Though not all novels can yield a complete reading in terms of architectural phenomenology, fictive architecture—in levels from landscape to artifact—makes up a substantial part of the representative content of nearly all fiction, simply because characters must and do function within some kind of *imago mundi.*

The particular importance of discussing Yoknapatawpha in this context is that the Faulkner canon offers an entire fictive county of substantial organic integrity, possessed of a complete hierarchy of natural and architectural forms, each of which function as representative elements in many and various ways. Each novel is a wholly different approach in fictive architecture:

The Unvanquished depicts the house as inspiration and representative image, and a vertical hierarchy of human postures on the landscape.

Absalom, Absalom! renders the house as a contrived image of didactic and coerced inspiration, possessed of a sentient *genius loci* which characterizes and interacts with its own inhabitants.

Sartoris deals with interior space as representative environment, the room as extension of the person, and the image of the town house in a small community.

Go Down, Moses posits a hierarchy of representative natural and man-made places on a landscape, and shows natural place as communicative person and sentient being.

The Snopes trilogy demonstrates a composed sequence of built structures as the register of personal gain, and the small town as a community in defense of its moral image.

Requiem for a Nun's interchapters are the folk history of the urban design of a fictive small town as an enactment of communal founding through the establishment of law.

Of the works not dealt with here, *As I Lay Dying* and *The Sound and the Fury* have been thoroughly considered by James Watson in his "Faulkner: The House of Fiction,"[1] which clearly explicates Addie's coffin as "half house and half bed," and the Bundren home as "both setting and symbol," from its emblematic site plan to its *genius loci,* whom Darl can see and hear.

As a presence, the *genius loci* of a dwelling, a district or a region is not only a palpable, sensible spirit but is often a conscious sentient one, almost a person. Sutpen's house is such a sentient spirit, knowing Henry's touch and step. The Wilderness is a sentient natural enclosure which responds with love for those who care for it. And Beat Four, the outland area of *Intruder,* is a place-become-person. It is first a domain; an area inhabited by people of one mind, with a two-dimensional attitude. Though Beat Four is named by a number like Sutpen's Hundred, it has no real consciousness like the house or the Big Woods. Yet, as Gavin infers (p. 59), it is the name of a collective person, a place with a name that can be called, addressed, a place that can be spoken to. When Lucas asks Gavin Stevens what he's going to do with him, Gavin replies, "Nothing. My name ain't Gowrie. It ain't even Beat Four." And later Gavin's frustration with Lucas leads him to say, "Tell the Gowries to never mind it when they bust in her tonight. Tell Beat Four to just forget it—" (p. 61).

The obverse of this place-become-person is the person who inhabits his mind as a place—he lives in his thoughts and reveries. In *The Sound and the Fury,* Faulkner's Quentin Compson is oblivious to the space he occupies, while his consciousness dwells more in the buildings of his mind. The above-mentioned essay by James Watson applies Bachelard's *Poetics of Space* to articulate the psychic fictive architecture of *The Sound and the Fury,* noting that Quentin "inhabits the [Compson] house in memory in nearly the same way as Ben does in fact."[2]

Literary criticism—that is to say the analysis and explication—of fictive architecture begins in phenomenology. The discussions in preceding chapters have appraised individual dwellings or man-made structures of many building types: mansion house and outbuildings, town house, dog-trot, church, and courthouse. The Sartoris house or the McCaslin place generate significance from a site plan or architectural floor plan. At the Sutpen and McCaslin houses details are important, as is the case at the Old Frenchman Place, where its legend contains the significance of its details. The details of both Sutpen's house and Snopes's mansion display the pretentiousness of the lives lived there.

Part of the significance of a house, a town, or a county may derive from what elements—what centers, paths, or enclosures—characterize it. The gravestone which Sutpen sets up in the hall of his house gives the hall a static character, makes it a contradiction of itself, and suggests the house's denial of its very purpose.

An entire range of built and unbuilt objects has been addressed, from the Sartoris gate, the MacCallums' clock, Narcissa's piano and Jefferson's lock to archetypal objects like the bed, the McCaslin table, and the Beauchamp hearth, as well as natural objects like the trees, the ground, and the river that compose the Yoknapatawpha wilderness. The two pulpits of *Light in August* might be mentioned in this regard, since it seems they are both usurped (by Christmas and Doc Hines) for purposes of cursing God or preaching unchristian lessons.

Architectural phenomenology has been used here not only to describe or appraise the nature of concrete things in fictive architecture, but also to address the nature of experiences such as an *aura,* Old Ben's domain, or the condition of dwelling and belonging. It has also been employed to examine the active personal response to the meaning of a place and acceptance of the responsibilities it involves.

In considering the nature of dwelling, the most surprising aspect which Faulkner's people exhibit is that those who dwell most fully are those without dwellings; V.K. Ratliff in his itinerancy, Ike McCaslin in the woods, and Lena Grove in her journeying. The stance and responses of Joe Christmas and Joanna Burden within her house and in her room, even the image of the old Burden place itself, are not as meaningful as Lena's presence within the small group of structures she inhabits.

Lena is searching not only for her husband, but for a home, a dwelling. She is the creator of community. On her father's trips to Doane's Mill during her young life, she descends from her father's wagon on the outskirts of town "because she believed that the people who saw her and whom she passed on foot would believe that she lived in the town too" (p. 3). That is, she wants to be seen as part of the community, as one who dwells in it. In terms of occupational dwelling, Lena advances from slow moving wagons to a boarding house, then to "the nearest thing to a home [Lucas] had ever or ever will have" (p. 274)—a dwelling. At the end of the novel she has the best of all three, so to speak: a house on wheels in which she is only boarding. But like V.K. Ratliff, she is at home anywhere she is. As a catalyst for community, she brings the Armstids closer together. Even her last name is a collective noun for a natural place, and goes with Bunch as representative of those who generate community. Her needs are simple and innocent, and the response of others to her needs is the central virtue of community: the practice of responding to the needs of others is something Byron finds easy and natural, and Hightower finds is necessary to be accepted among his community.

Beyond objects, structures, places, and various conditions, a phenomenological approach may also be applied to the fictive occurrence of basic elemental substances. Some situations, for instance (particularly in *The Mansion* and *Intruder in the Dust*), center on the ground of significance for all natural and man-made places, the Earth. In the case of *Intruder,* the violation of the Gowrie grave is a violation of sacred place. And when graves are put where they are not intended, the Earth itself is violated.

Earth is the most fundamental of elements. If stone is the most inevitable thing on Earth, earth itself is the most ubiquitous, the most eternal, the most moderate of inanimate things. *Land* is earth *in principle:* it is earth designated, deeded and owned, belonged to. The tenant farmer and the sharecropper are owned by the land. The *ground,* or the earth as Mink feels it in the conclusion of *The Mansion* (pp. 402–3), is the horizontal surface we live on, walk on—the plane of the Earth, that is (*Mansion,* p. 435), not the globe—which we never pass through until we die. *Soil* is the rich earth, *dirt* the poor earth, the "sworn foe and mortal enemy" of "every tenant farmer and sharecropper" (*Mansion,* p. 90). *Sod* is earth with plant life within it. *Mud* is the too-abundant earth, the earth gone soft. *Dust* is the dry earth, worthless, dispersed, and unformable; and *sand* is the most undependable, without permanence or stability. *Quicksand* is the most treacherous of earth. Worse than being unreliable or unstable, it is ravenously subtractive. Things are not built on quicksand, but concealed within it. Nor are things given to quicksand as you give things to earth. What is given to the earth nourishes it, but what is given to quicksand is taken by it to be concealed. Quicksand is the opposite of the earth to which the beloved are interred, and this is the source of Miss Habersham's disdain of Crawford Gowrie. What compounds Crawford's fratricide for her is that to cover the evidence he committed his brother's body not back to the loving earth, but to the perverse and devious quicksand. Even the mud along the branch bank keeps the prints of Crawford and his mule long enough to lead the sheriff and his party to the evidence. And the shaled earth of the pitifully shallow grave where Jake Montgomery is buried reveals Crawford's "frantic hand-to-hand combat with the massy intolerable inertia of the earth itself" (*Intruder,* p. 174). The earth cannot fool or be fooled, and it will not cover a trail or hide transgressions. But quicksand is secretive: it is earth that is feared even by animals, as Highboy shows in shying away from the bank on his first approach with Aleck Sander. In short, quicksand is the negative of earth, earth as a vacuum.

Finally, the study of imaginative place in Yoknapatawpha discloses a range of levels to fictive architecture, each of which handles certain relationships:

The fictive room, or enclosed place, articulates the individual character and often the most intimate details of his person. It renders man as either alone with himself, alone among the things which are his, or as intimate with one other.

The fictive dwelling, from mansion to cabin, depicts a larger-scale relationship in concretizing the significance of the family and of individual protagonists who dwell within it. Whatever the magnitude of its public meaning (and it may render an individual or communal relationship by its locale), the fictive house also expresses meaning through the interrelationships of its interior spaces and in the furniture and details it encloses. It renders man under his roof within his family and may express his place within the community as well.

Fictive townscapes concretize relationships between the inhabitants of a community and the community itself as the commonweal. The rendering emphasizes a collection of individual structures and the interaction of individuals among these structures, as well as their accomplishments as a community. This level renders man in his district among his neighbors, is generically comic and affirms the continuity of communal existence, though the rendering of town founding may suggest an epic action.

Fictive landscape forms usually represent broader universal ideas than either individual character, family, or community (though some individuals dwelling on the landscape may participate more intensely in the significance embodied in it, or may have a particularly intimate relationship to the landscape). They render man's most fundamental position of being, as Norberg-Schulz would say, "on the earth and under the sky." Their meanings are largely lyrical and idyllic, sometimes pastoral. The image of mule, plow, and man which Chick Mallison sees in *Intruder* (animal, machine, and man on equal terms, without hierarchy or stratification), is an image of man on the landscape, an image of agrarian life as a concretization of the South, "the land's living symbol."[3]

As difficult as it is to manage large pieces of fictive territory, there is another larger scale—the largest in fact—available to the novelist: imaginative space at the astrosophical level, or fictive cosmic space. The preextant world created by the author is and often must be complete to the stars. Faulkner's exercise of this scale occurs in his occasional references to the slowly wheeling stars overhead. Whether invoked by a protagonist such as Gavin Stevens in his "There is a ridge" soliloquy in *The Town,* or by the author himself, as in the later part of *Requiem,* the perception of man on the earth and under the stars is a glimpse of him as an inhabitant of the cosmos,[4] a vision of the human condition as a whole against the background of the infinite reaches of the cosmos. Its purpose is to address again the timeless question of the telos— whether things are indeed moving towards completion.

Though such a perspective—from the opposite end of the telescope, as it were—would seem to stress the insignificance of man in the vast labyrinth of galactic scale interstellar space, Faulkner's depiction of his characters as inhabitants of cosmological space is an affirmative rendering, his cosmos is teleologically ordered. When Sarty Snopes sits on the hill beneath the wheeling stars at the conclusion of "Barn Burning," he is an inhabitant of the cosmos, and the evidence that he is where he should be and that all things are working towards completion is the slow wheeling of the stars over his head. At the close of *The Mansion,* after Gavin and Ratliff have tended to their last business of securing Mink's escape, they come out of the ruins of Mink's old dwelling as "the constellations wheeled through the zodiacal pastures" (T, p. 312). More than the slow wheeling constellations of "Barn Burning," this syntagm is a compaction of four ideas. The noun "constellations" establishes that the subject is the stars, but these are collections of stars in shapes understood by the human eye. The verb "wheeled" engages the metaphor of the celestial clock and suggests the slow and certain march of time that measures teleological motion. The naming of the zodiac ensures the involvement of Fate and the certitude of its workings. And finally, the mention of "pastures" points to fulfillment concretized in a landscape image which Mink can understand. Its meaning is that the motion of the stars measures out the slow but inevitable process by which Fate brings all things to fulfillment in terms all those involved might understand.[5]

Though a certain sardonic tone may color this distant perspective upon the human effort at dwelling on this small planet—as it does in Faulkner's near-bombastic remarks in the later chapters of *Requiem* (p. 247), or Gavin's monologue in *The Town* (pp. 315–17)—Faulkner's cosmological space is ordered, guided, and telic. As "Barn Burning" closes, morning will come and Sarty will stand and walk down the hill into a new life and a new space, the significance of which is crystallized by his decision to act for the good. But just now the slow completion of this part of his life is concretized in the wheeling stars of cosmological space.

As the concluding narrator of *The Mansion* steps back to show Gavin, Ratliff, and Mink under the same wheeling stars, Mink rests for a few moments in celestial time. Later, on or under the earth, Mink may begin another cycle, in a different place, a different landscape, even a different region, but in the same cosmological space. And the completion of this cycle is concretized in the same wheeling stars.

In considering the scope of imaginative place we may think of cosmological space as one kind of cognitive space, for it is space we can only think about and not existentially dwell in.[6] In fiction, however, cosmological space becomes a form of expressive or artistic space, and the *imago mundi* becomes an image of the cosmos. At its fundamental point of significance, fictive architecture is symbolic in the same way that substantial architecture is: it concretizes meanings which it gathers to itself, and in turn reveals or expresses these meanings to those who dwell within and around it.

In *Genius Loci,* Norberg-Schulz writes that "things always tell several stories; they tell about their own making, they tell about the historical circumstances under which they were made, and if they are real things, they also reveal truth" (p. 185). What might be said of fictive architecture is only slightly different. The natural and man-made places of fiction participate in the telling of the story. Although they tell about the historical circumstances of their creation (the author's milieu), this is not their most important function. They concretize meanings within the story as well as the *genius loci* of the fictive envelope, and so participate in the reality they represent. But the other truth they reveal is a truth about poetry; imagined places are also real things and reveal truth in the meanings they concretize. By reading, knowing, and witnessing to the significances of both fictive and actual natural and man-made places, men can dwell fully—that is to say poetically—in the world.

Appendix

The Tradition of Southern Classicism

Faulkner's fictive county was wrought out of a geographical reality, part of an entire region possessing a certain homogeneity in its cultural values. Though the validity of Yoknapatawpha is in no way dependent on its correspondence with the geographical reality of Lafayette County, the *genius loci* of the region to which both belong is important background for a complete understanding of the *genius loci* of Faulkner's imaginative world. The unique attitude with which the American South witnesses to its cultural values and perceives its *genius loci* cultural analysts are often wont to call the Southern mind.[1] The central core of this homogeneous body of values which informs the *genius loci* of the American South is composed primarily of the Classical convictions central to its working beliefs. In the words of Richard Weaver,

> no account of the mind of the South can be valid unless it stresses the extent to which the Southerner is classical man. Even in the South of today one can find surviving large segments of the classical-Christian-medieval synthesis. It is not unusual for a Southerner of the upper class to steep himself in Roman history and name his sons after Roman generals. Here the Greek Revival in architecture had its inception; and here, in the region influenced by Charleston, the idea of Greek democracy was not only practiced but articulated in theory, as Vernon Parrington demonstrated in his great work on American culture.[2]

A considerably more succinct and in some ways better comment is Francis Pendleton Gaines's remark that many writers "have claimed for this social order the philosophical tone of Greece, the dominant political energy of Rome, and the beauty of chivalry softened by the spiritual quality of Christianity."[3] Although a studied comparison of the South and the Classical world is hardly to be found,[4] there is in the writings of its cultural historians consistent and ample evidence of the region's Hellenic and Hellenistic sources and origins, from which it is possible to assemble a cultural profile of the South.[5] From Weaver's comment on the Southerner as Classical man it is a short step to Frank Owsley's related remarks on the origins of the agrarian tradition in the South of the early Republic. In "The Irrepressible Conflict" he writes:

Men so loved their life upon the soil that they sought out in literature and history peoples who had lived in a similar life, so that they might justify and further stimulate their own concepts of life and perhaps set a high goal for themselves among the great nations which had sprung from the land.... [T]he even-poised and leisurely life of the Greeks, their oratory, their philosophy, their art—especially their architecture—appealed to the South. The Greek tradition became partly grafted upon the Anglo-Saxon and Scotch tradition of life. However, it was the Romans of the early Republic... who appealed most powerfully to the South. ... they had wrestled with virgin soil and forests; they could build log houses and were closer to many Southerners than even the English gentleman in his moss-covered stone house. It was Cincinnatus, whose hands were rough with guiding the plow, rather than Cato, who wrote about Roman agriculture and lived in a villa, whom Southerners admired the most, though they read and admired Cato as a fine gentleman with liberal ideas about tenants and slaves and a thorough knowledge and love of the soil.[6]

The perspectives of these two senior cultural historians indicate the twofold Greek and Roman nature of the Southern Classical tradition: Greek art and philosophy on the one hand, and the Roman agrarian tradition on the other as the source of the Southerner's love for the land.[7] Both Weaver and Owsley mention Greek philosophy, oratory, rhetoric, art, and architecture, but the difference is one of emphasis. Owsley, the champion of the yeoman farmer (whose heroes were the Gracchi), quite naturally sees the Roman agrarian tradition as dominant. But it is Weaver who, while recognizing the importance of history to both civilizations, sees the humanistic pursuits of art and philosophy as the true registers of cultural values and beliefs. The many similarities between the South and ancient Greece are cultural and spiritual rather than historical or chronological. Where the South does not conform to Greek *paideia* it usually remains within the temper of ancient Rome and hence within the Classical tradition.

Southern political philosophy seems best known for its stand on states' rights and sovereignty, a posture almost antifederal in its advocation of a weak central government in favor of close association with and allegiance to local rule. Although the principle of states' rights is generally thought to have arisen among the issues of the time (and in the oratory) of John C. Calhoun, this and other fundamentally Greek principles of Southern political philosophy are rooted in the Founding influence of Colonial Virginia.[8]

The coexistence of states' rights and sovereignty with confederational politics was as much a reflection of familially structured society as was the Southern practice of patriarchal governance.

The basis of all society, of course, and the fundamental unit of community is the family, and the Southern understanding of family—what it is and what it means—was in itself the ground of all forms of personal and public relationship. Both Southern and Trojan societies were patriarchal, where the first commandment, though unwritten, was "Honor thy father, his precepts, his heritage and his legacy." The sons of aristocrat and yeoman alike saw their grandfathers as repositories of the knowledge and skill of long experience and reflection and felt that age brought "wisdom rather than senility."[9] These notions of family were not consciously derived from those of ancient societies, but were a natural recurrence of them, and the Southerner out of love for his ancestor and respect for his wisdom, continued to hold him in the Trojan *pater familias* tradition; as lord of the household and head of the family he was entitled to domestic veneration. Like Voegelin's Roman, the Southerner felt that "the 'family was immortal'; the business of its members, while they live, being to 'carry the person' of the family, showing themselves worthy representatives of the ancestors whose names they bear."[10]

Fundamentally, the South was a unified community. The independence of each state, fostered by the autonomy of the individual plantations within them, was balanced by a Greek sense of regional bonds among the people, by which the South knew itself as one blood-related community, like Troy. The Greek polis carried familial implications or, as Cochrane says, "an all-in partnership"; and the South's sense of community was fundamentally the same as that which engendered the Hellenic polis. The often mentioned distinction between individual and community usually attributed to the Greeks was actually unknown to the Hellenes and only developed later in Hellenistic Greece and Rome.[11] The Southern sense of community was a species of this more compact earlier Hellenic understanding, paradoxically balanced by a Roman distinction between public and private which had never been so customarily observed since the days of *res publica* and *res privata*.

But the South was hardly political in the Aristotelian sense. Its notions of family and patriarchal guidance moved in a Greek way from the private over to the public realm and informed the political structure.[12] The Southern understanding of political community, thus, was not only derived from Greek political philosophers and the Bible, as M.E. Bradford says, but from basic familial piety as well.[13]

The political order of the South can be extracted from Leveque's description of the Achaean order: like Greece it was ruled by groups of local nobles, large landowners who had obtained most of the best farming land. In the South these were, in a less formal way, what the council was in the aristocratic regimes of early Greece, such as in Corinth:[14] a corporate body made up of the heads of great families. "Achaean Greece," Leveque notes, "emerges as divided into a number of autonomous realms, each grouped around a fortified manor."[15] Even the word polis, he tells us, originally designated a citadel.[16] The political notion of states' rights is doubtless rooted in the local autonomy enjoyed by these individual plantation estates, an autonomy not unlike that of Attic Greece. Though these large domains had to make certain concessions to state administration,[17] each realm enjoyed a certain independence, and their size and remoteness encouraged such autonomy, practiced under the Aristotelian understanding "that Justice is without application . . . where there are 'no common magistracies to enforce engagements'. . . . "[18] A certain communal self-sufficiency complemented and probably often preceded this autonomy, for personal as well as communal self-sufficiency were deep-seated beliefs for both Greek and Southerner.[19] Now and then, however, under extreme conditions such as war,[20] and united by a common interest, they would form a confederational community in defense against a common foe. In time of war, both the South and Attic Greece formed a confederacy and called itself one, united by common interest and acknowledging a common leader.[21] Among others, Bradley T. Johnson has remarked on the similarity of Southern political events to those of the ancient world: "There was forming in the South a military democracy, aggressive, ambitious, intellectual and brave, such as led Athens in her brightest epoch and controlled Rome in her most glamorous days."[22]

In sum, the nature of the *koina* of both the South and Attic Greece suggests that the South was what Leveque calls an *amphictyony;* a collection of poleis with certain geographical, ethnic, religious and economic characteristics which held it together as a region.[23] More specifically, and more importantly, the South became in essence a federated ethnos; the sociopolitical form the polis becomes when it enters into a confederation. Though a political history of the Confederacy is out of place here, it is important to note that the American South, like Attic Greece, sought for a period of about seventy years to establish a limited, well-defined communal society in a political arena principally concerned with empire politics. Like fourth-century Athens, the American South participated little in colonization, seeking rather to work its way deep into its own fertile southwest and remain there, while the rest of the nation pursued expansion into what seemed a limitless frontier. Southerners may rightfully think of themselves when Cochrane says that the Greeks "had struggled to raise themselves from the level of surrounding barbarism and to construct out of available materials a world corresponding to what they conceived to be the true potential of humanity."[24] As a people Southerners were, as Isocrates said of the Hellenes, not a race but an intelligence[25] and may be compared to the Northern states as Greece might be compared to Rome, China to Japan, or England to America. Greece built a culture based on traditional values; Rome built a civilization on its technology.

Though the South was not constitutionally aristocratic in its political structure, it was socially comparable to aristocratic Greece after the reform of Cleisthenes. This social aristocracy was informed with the same political imperative for governance over the less competent[26] that Bowra attributes to Attic Greece: "though the aristocratic life was confined to a few, it solidified Greek civilization and gave a special pattern to it. Those who enjoyed its liberties were expected to shoulder the responsibility for maintaining them, and their respect for individuality was guaranteed by the same social frame which held it."[27]

The inward and active form of political energy took the form of a sense of civic obligation. From Cicero the Southern patrician knew, in Cochrane's words, that life was "a complex of obligations to oneself and others, in the discharge of which a man realizes the fullest potentialities of his being."[28] The obligations themselves however, the contents of those responsibilities, were articulated from Greek sources,[29] though the personal paradigm was drawn from the Roman political person. "Many of [William] Wirt's contemporaries," William Taylor tells us, "thought they saw in Roman politics under the Republic the perfection of civil government. Then more than at any time in history, they felt, the affairs of men rested in the hands of high-minded and decorus patricians who conducted their business and settled their differences rationally and with eloquence."[30] This is the identical spirit which Vernon Parrington describes as "the aristocratic spirit of the Old Dominion... tempered by the feeling of patriarchal responsibility, and... an admirable republican squirarchy."[31] It is the core of the notion of patriarchal governance and the point at which such governance meets the Greek ideal of democracy recovered by John Calhoun. Parrington's definition argues that "Democracy is possible only in a society that recognizes inequality as a law of nature, but in which the virtuous and capable enter into a voluntary co-partnership for the common good, accepting wardship of the incompetent in the interest of society. This was the Greek ideal and this ideal had created Greek civilization."[32] A natural consequence of this sense of responsibility was an attraction towards the profession of law, which became for most Southerners an avocation. Taylor notes that the older South's "more oratorical tradition... looked upon the law, not as a lucrative business, but as a preparation for statesmanship and high-minded public service. 'The profession of law in this country,' one of them commented, 'involves the cultivation of eloquence, and leads to political advancement and public honors. In this respect we nearly resemble the Roman Republic.'"[33] The other half of Southern political consciousness, then, was an awareness of itself as part of a Roman style republic with a patrician government which exhibited the legalism, rhetoric, and oratory of Republican Rome.[34]

The Classical Christian genius of the South was apparent too in its social structure, again primarily Greek and only secondarily Roman. Though class lines were far less strictly defined than those in Europe,[35] the structure was composed of groups of freemen roughly comparable to those of fifth-century Athens: there were Tidewater landowners and merchants like the *Paraloi* (coastal peoples concerned with commerce), upcountry and inland alluvial landowners like the *Pediakoi*, and yeomen hill farmers like the *Diakrioi* (led by Pisistratus, the Jacksonian of his day).[36] This topographically grouped social structure was far more rigid in fifth-century Athens than in the American South, where the various elements lived side by side on the landscape, rather like Periclean society.

Yeoman and planter shared belief in what may be called the social religion of the South, which seeks wisdom by contemplation in the knowledge that man is an imperfectable and fallen creature. The Southerner's reverence for mystery and discount of pure reason characterized his religious thinking and inspired a Vergilian kind of "thinking with the blood."[37] The Southerner views his religion as he views history, i.e., as a set of images to contemplate.[38] His understanding of the truth of myth is not unlike the ancient Greek's; the authenticity of the story is not as important as the truth it reveals. In no way is this approach dispassionate. The South, writes Richard Weaver, "retains a belief that religion is the expression of man's poetic, tragic, and metaphysical intuitions of life, and that as such religion is tied neither to science nor utility."[39] Understanding is thus reached by the aforementioned contemplation of the myth,[40] which cultivates restraint and a generally settled quality about one's faith,[41] unquestioned belief in established doctrine, an acceptance of mystery, and a willingness to abide by the tradition. Southern religiousness has been described as the older religiousness of Greece in the age of the ancient mysteries of Eleusis: "belief in a revealed knowledge is the essence of religion in the older sense."[42] Its focal virtue is *pietas*, a piety for the natural world and the mysteries it holds, a piety freely given out of a settled mind.[43] Such a virtue allows for clearer and quicker understanding of the meaning of natural space and place. Like his cultural ancestor in Creto-Mycenaean civilization, the Southerner is continually attuned to "the mysterious presences which motivated natural life."[44] The pious acceptance of nature and its inscrutability leads outward to an acceptance of the order of the universe.

In matters of its public orthodoxy[45] the South was, again, a complex of Classical views, predominantly Greek. Although it cherished the Trojan tradition of *pater familias* and a belief in the Godhead as the traditional God, the God of our fathers, the Southern mind held the early Greek view that the gods precede the city as nature precedes political philosophy, rather than the Northern and Roman view that the founding of the city (on the Hill) establishes the institution of its gods. The argument of Cicero notwithstanding—that we carried our household gods from falling Troy (or Europe) and instituted them in the shrines and groves of the city to bless and insure good fortune for our state—the Southerner believed with the Greeks that the gods—*the* God—was always here, in the ancient fables and creation myths, preceding our civic existence. The South's was, as Richard Weaver has said, the older religiousness, "one of unquestioned and unquestionable supports of the general settlement under which men live."[46] Political order was based on the precepts of the Natural Law, its precedence to human law, and the idea that the polis was the family writ large.

Though virtuous action seemed to promote the continuity of political order, the Civil War forced the South to accept, still gracefully and with honor, the evident hiatus between virtue and fortune. This acceptance was aided not only by the submissive quality of its faith, but also by the image of Troy which history itself gave as an analog for contemplation.

Few, if any, civilizations have as many parallels to Classical history as does the American South. Not only was the Southerner's view of history, elaborated earlier, similar to that of the men who instituted its study, but like any contemporary of Herodotus, he felt he could be a part of his own history and knew the history that his ancestors made.[47] Other writers than John William de Forest have maintained that Southerners were "as different from other Americans as the ancient Spartans from the Athenians."[48] One of the most sustained if less sincere parallels is Gildersleeve's, on which Richard Weaver elaborates:

> "A Southerner in the Peloponnesian War," a half-serious comparison of the American civil conflict with the famous war of antiquity, follows the truism that all wars are one war. Gildersleeve proceeded to show how the American struggle could be described down to astonishingly small details in the language of Thucydides. The ancient affair was "a war between two leagues, a Northern Union and a Southern Confederacy. The Northern Union, represented by Athens, was a naval power; the Southern Confederacy under the leadership of Sparta, was a land power. The Athenians represented the progressive element, the Spartans the conservative. The Athenians believed in a strong centralized government. The Lacedaemonians professed in a greater regard for autonomy."[49]

Though other Spartan/Greek historical similarities appear in the ideas of inherited government and peacetime concentration of power in the hands of landed proprietors,[50] Donald Davidson, in response to W.J. Cash's over-generalized gloss of the Southern mind, denies that the South was either Dorian or Spartan.[51] Still other similarities, however, persist. The movement toward constitutional government by the First Families of the Old Dominion is broadly comparable to the movement from patriarchal rule to the order of *Dike*, the order of written laws, in seventh-century Greece, or to the coming of Cleisthenian democratic reforms after Isagoras's attempts to maintain oligarchy in Athens.[52]

The closest parallels of course come, however sadly, in the wars suffered by both cultures; and the frequency of allusion to Troy in Southern poetry and literature is not without justification. Though the primary political referent before the war was Athens, there was often emphasis on the image of Troy as a community and reference to Aeneas's Rome as the providential realization of an ideal order.[53] After the war the fall of Troy was the most natural and appropriate of analogs,[54] while the cultural remnant of the South which survived also alluded to the Athens that emerged from the Peloponnesian War as a defeated power and a crippled culture. Postbellum Southerners contemplated and submitted to Reconstruction as a kind of parallel to the subjugation of Athens by Sparta. From study of the Persian Wars, Southerners saw that both commonwealths were attacked by northern invaders, defended themselves valiantly, and suffered sacking. The subsequent triumph of Athens and its unification of the various regions into a confederation, however, belong in this comparison to antebellum Southern history. After the formation of the league of Delos, Athens emerged as the kind of unified humanistic cultural community which the South emulated from 1830 to 1860. It is the Athens after the Peloponnesian War that compares, especially in its effects, with post-Civil War Dixie. Like the Athenian confederacy, the South reached a cultural high point from which it had to fight a war to defend its independence, lost that war, and was forever broken, not only from the defeat, but from the energy, resources, and manpower put into its defense.[55] The effects of the Peloponnesian War on the agriculture of the region, as detailed by Leveque, read much the same as those of the Civil War on the South:

> [The war] brought perpetual mobilization of agriculturists in its wake, had ruined agriculture and, worse still, destroyed the social class of small and medium landowners. Recreated by Solon and developed by Pisistratus, this class had made up the strength of Periclean Athens, giving it political stability and supplying it with excellent hoplites, hardened by work in the field and completely devoted to their native land. When the war had ended and woefully so, many of them did not have the heart to rehabilitate their ravaged fields.... This was the sempiternal movement of the flight to the town by the broken peasant, selling up his possessions in the hope of a less wretched life. Mortgage posts multiplied in the Attic countryside.... Aristocrats or more often *nouveaux riches* built up vast estates, glad to invest part of their fortune in landed property, all the more so as rational farming often proved very lucrative.... The rich worked their lands by means of day-labourers, often the former dispossessed owners of the soil....[56]

The American South holds other distinctly Classical attributes, most of which reside in the individual Southern person than in political or social effort. Concerning the character of the gentleman patriarchy, it may be said that the imperative of patriarchal governance was no more than an extension of the tradition of patriarchal maintenance of the moral norm of the community,[57] affirmed by the First Families of Virginia. They consulted Classical sources not only as examples of proper conduct, but for examples on how to instruct others.[58] The literature written by the *antebellum* Southerner derived its *genre* as well from Classical models: There was biography as exemplar, after Plutarch, character sketches like those by Byrd,[59] after Theophrastus, and history in justification after Heroditus.[60]

Among other attributes of the gentleman patriarch was a deep understanding of the purpose of leisure which provided, as already mentioned, the atmosphere for the contemplative part of existence. One Classical reference to leisure is architectural, for Leveque sees the Greek sense of leisure reflected in its urban design: "There is no better evidence of the prosperity of the Greek world and the leisure its inhabitants enjoyed than these harmonious towns, where all was order and beauty—on the agora, at the theatre and palaestra, and even in the most utilitarian buildings."[61]

Other Classical similarities might be elaborated here, among them the notion of the good life, the tradition of taste and elegance not unlike that maintained by the Alcmaeonids,[62] a pride of place and ancestry,[63] and the aristocratic morality of its leaders.[64] All of these are part of the content of the Classical *genius loci* of the South, and as such are part of the thoughts and feelings that animate the reactions of Faulkner's people to the county and region in which they dwell. The architectural aspects are, of course, the most important, and it is these which are most important to this study.

Notes

Introduction

1. The foremost phenomenologist of architecture, Christian Norberg-Schulz, insists throughout his book *Genius Loci: Towards a Phenomenology of Architecture* (New York: Rizzoli, 1980) that part of this basic human need is the need to understand the meaning of both natural and man-made places. See *Genius Loci*, pp. 23, 166, 180.

2. Martin Heidegger has much to say about the creative imagination in his *Poetry, Language, Thought* (New York: Harper and Row, 1975).

3. It is because "dwelling is the manner in which mortals *are* on the earth," Heidegger says, that we are dwellers first and builders second; "We do not dwell because we have built, but we build...because we dwell" (from "Building Dwelling Thinking," in *Poetry, Language, Thought*, p. 148).

4. Man creates space "to express the structure of his world as a real *imago mundi*. We may call this creation expressive or artistic space.... In a certain sense, any man who chooses a place in his environment to settle and live, is a creator of expressive space." (Norberg-Schulz, *Existence, Space and Architecture* [New York: Praeger, 1971], p. 11).

5. Norberg-Schulz, *Existence*, p. 11. Space must be understood here "as an existential dimension, as a relation between man and his environment...as a dimension of human existence, rather than as a dimension of thought or perception" (*Existence*, p. 14).

6. In delineating the nature of architectural space, Norberg-Schulz says, "we do not here distinguish between 'natural' and man-made elements in the environment. What man *selects* from nature to serve his purposes, we also call 'architecture'" (*Existence*, p. 37, n.1).

7. Richard Gill, *Happy Rural Seat: The English Country House and the Literary Imagination* (New Haven: Yale University Press, 1972). The English manor-house novel and its tradition are paralleled in New England, Gill notes, by Hawthorne, among others. In the American South, the tradition continued in the form of the plantation novel, about which more will be said later.

8. The analysis which follows is an application of Christian Norberg-Schulz's phenomenology of architecture, as articulated in *Genius Loci*, to the phenomenon of fictive architecture.

9. Yi-Fu Tuan, *Topophilia: A Study of Environmental Perception, Attitudes, and Values* (Englewood Cliffs, N.J.: Prentice-Hall, 1974), pp. 49–50.

10. Norberg-Schulz, *Existence*, pp. 30–31.

11. Norberg-Schulz, *Existence*, p. 31.

12. See Norberg-Schulz, *Intentions in Architecture* (Cambridge: MIT Press, 1965), p. 173.

13. See this author's " 'Like between Two Teams of Horses': Snopes and Sartoris in 'Barn Burning' " (University of Dallas master's thesis, 1970).

14. The complementary situation to this home-as-public-building is the public building as "the home of a well-defined community." See Norberg-Schulz, *Existence*, p. 88.

15. "Stairways to the cellar are usually hidden from public view, while stairways to the upper levels of the house range from modest to elegant dramatizations of the more noble activity of ascending to, or decending from, the heavens" (Kent C. Bloomer and Charles W. Moore, *Body, Memory, and Architecture* [New Haven: Yale University Press, 1977], p. 48).

    The private actions of our existence are performed in the higher and separate parts of the house. In the old Tennessee house Cragfront, for example, the second floor front section, which holds the bedrooms, is not accessible from the second floor ballroom. Private and public distinctions are maintained. The Classical authority for this is Vitruvius, Book VI, chapter 5, p. 181. The dog-trot house, with its lower-floor main bedroom, does not belie this point, since the yeoman farmer is a more private person than his low-country neighbor. The public-private distinction causes much family embarrassment in Eudora Welty's *Delta Wedding* (New York: Harcourt, Brace, 1945), p. 138, when Robbie cries in the most public of places.

16. Norberg-Schulz, *Existence*, pp. 88–95.

17. See Norberg-Schulz, *Existence*, pp. 98–103.

18. Correct criticism respects the fictive nature of the world Faulkner creates and understands the distinction between the fictive world presupposed by the writer and antecedent to his characters, and the factual world inhabited by the author himself, a part of the region from which he draws his fictive world. In the case of Yoknapatawpha and Lafayette counties, of course, the task is much more difficult owing to the close similarity of the two environments, one imaginary and one not. For remark on the errant and correct approaches to Faulkner's fictive county, see Noel Polk's review of Elizabeth Kerr's book *Yoknapatawpha: Faulkner's 'Little Postage Stamp of Native Soil'* (New York: Fordam University Press, 1976), in "The Critics and Faulkner's 'Little Postage Stamp of Native Soil,' " *Mississippi Quarterly* 23 (1970): 323–35.

    Though Ms. Kerr's monograph dedicates an entire chapter to the fictive county, detailing its topography by quadrants and describing its built forms, it should be read after Calvin Brown's homespun but authoritative "Faulkner's Geography and Topography," an appendix to his *A Glossary of Faulkner's South* (New Haven: Yale University Press, 1976), pp. 223–41. Charles S. Aiken's "Faulkner's Yoknapatawpha County: A Place in the American South," *Geographical Review* 69 (July, 1979): 331–48, even in its ethnic studies and fictive demographics, is a good course correction from his earlier "Faulkner's Yoknapatawpha County: Geographical Fact into Fiction," *Geographical Review* 67 (January, 1977): 1–21, and affirms that Yoknapatawpha needs no geographical certification, nor is it invalidated by conflicting details from the real northern Mississippi.

    Shorter studies of Faulkner's fictive architecture range widely in their validity. Two successful examinations of his imaginative structures are Noel Polk's "Alec Holston's Lock and the Founding of Jefferson," *Mississippi Quarterly* 24 (1971): 247–70, and Allen Gates's "The Old Frenchman Place: Symbol of a Lost Civilization," *Iowa English Yearbook* 13 (1968): 44–50. James G. Watson's "Faulkner: The House of Fiction" in *Fifty Years of Yoknapatawpha: Faulkner and Yoknapatawpha, 1979*, ed. Doreen Fowler and Ann J.

Abadie (Jackson: University Press of Mississippi, 1980), pp. 134–58, makes deft use of Bachelard's *Poetics of Space* in a superb study of houses and rooms in *As I Lay Dying* and *The Sound and the Fury*, especially the places in Quentin's mind. Another essay, John K. Crane's "The Jefferson Court House: An *Axis Exsecrabilis Mundi*," *Twentieth Century Literature* 15 (1969): 19–23, studies this centripetal structure in the light of Mircea Eliade's archetypal cosmology. But even the most intriguing of Yoknapatawpha's built forms, the mansions, are studied only in Gates's article and in Mark Allister's "Faulkner's Aristocratic Families: The Grand Design and the Plantation House," *Midwest Quarterly* 25 (1983): 90–101; an essay which does little else than note Faulkner's apparent change of attitude toward his mansions after 1935. Both are overshadowed by Guy A. Cardwell's "The Plantation House: An Analogical Image," *Southern Literary Journal* 2 (1969): 3–21, a broad study of the recurrence of this image in Southern literature which considers "The South" to be Faulkner's main theme rather than the region from which he drew his fictive world. Elmo Howell's "Faulkner's Country Church: A Note on 'Shingles for the Lord,'" *Mississippi Quarterly* 21 (1968): 205–10, is of some interest, but Robert M. Slabey's "Faulkner's Geography and Hightower's House," *American Notes and Queries* 3 (1965): 85–86, is only a brief remark. Richard E. Fisher's "The Wilderness, the Commissary, and the Bedroom: Faulkner's Ike McCaslin as Hero in a Vacuum," *English Studies* 44 (1963): 19–28, has little to do with landscape, built structure, or enclosure; it returns to the over-argued matter of Ike and his inheritance of the miscegenation curse.

19. See Allen Tate's *Essays of Four Decades* (Chicago: Swallow Press, 1968), pp. 558–76, where he says that Southerners "knew no history for the sake of knowing it, but simply for the sake of contemplating it and seeing in it an image of themselves." Hugh McGehee, the protagonist of Stark Young's *So Red the Rose* (New York: Scribner's, 1934), explains to his son that "our ideas and instincts work upon our memory of [our predecessors], and so they take on some clarity of outline" (p. 150).

20. Jay B. Hubbell, *Southern Life in Fiction* (Athens, Georgia: University of Georgia Press, 1960), pp. 11–12. See too Andrew Lytle's essay "Image as Guide to Meaning in the Historical Novel," in his *The Hero with the Private Parts* (Baton Rouge: Louisiana State University Press, 1966), pp. 5–20, and Donald Davidson's "Theme and Method in *So Red the Rose*," in his *Still Rebels, Still Yankees* (Baton Rouge: Louisiana State University Press, 1957).

21. A discussion of the Classical nature of the Southern *genius loci* is peripherally important to an understanding of Faulkner's fictive architecture. See the appendix to this study.

Chapter 1

1. The affinity of the Southern mind to Greek classical thinking has much to say about both the *genius loci* of the South and that of Faulkner's fictive county as well. For a discussion of the characteristics, convictions, and beliefs that make the American South the last Classical Christian cultural synthesis, see the appendix to this work.

2. Sigfried Giedion, the senior scholar of architecture and space in the history of human order, states that the Greek mind, discoverer of philosophical consciousness, "filled the landscape with psychic and religious meaning: they gave a spiritual import to rock, mountains, and sea.... nature was given a spiritualized human content." See *Architecture and the Phenomenon of Transition: The Three Space Concepts in Architecture* (Cambridge: Harvard University Press, 1971), pp. 8–9.

3. Christian Norberg-Schulz, *Genius Loci: Towards a Phenomenology of Architecture* (New York: Rizzoli, 1980), p. 45. Two other kinds of archetypal natural place are the Romantic and the Cosmic landscape.

4. The attitude is best exemplified in excerpts from an essay by Donald Davidson (in *Still Rebels, Still Yankees* [Baton Rouge: Louisiana State University Press, 1957], pp. 232, 239, 240) comparing the landscapes of Vermont and Georgia: "the trim Vermont fields where all the weeds were flowers and all the grass was hay. ... the very wilderness, in this New England state, had uprightness and order. ... In the clearings the farmhouses were all painted; and the barns were painted, too. The streams were orthodox streams, almost model streams, with water always translucent and stones rounded and picturesquely placed among moss and ferns. ... The Georgia landscape had a serene repose that lulled a man out of all need of conscience. It was anything but swept and garnished. It could be either mild or majestic or genial or savage depending on what view you got of pines against the red earth, or Negro cabins underneath their chinaberry trees, or sedge grass running into gullies and thence to impenetrable swamps, or deserted mansions lost in oak groves and magnolias. Rivers were muddy and at times unrestrained; they got out of bounds, as all things natural did here. ... The New Englander knew exactly where to find nature harsh and nature yielding, and he could make his arrangements accordingly. But the Georgian never knew. His safest policy was to relax, and he readily developed a great degree of tolerance for irregularity in nature and man."

5. Christian Norberg-Schulz, *Existence, Space and Architecture* (New York: Praeger, 1971), p. 61. See also Giedion, *Architecture and the Phenomenon of Transition*, p. 14.

6. Pierre Leveque notes in his *The Greek Adventure* (London: Weidenfeld and Nicolson, 1968) that the Archaic period included the birth of religious architecture. But it is Ulrich B. Phillips who remarked on Southern homesteads: "Columns plain or fluted, round or square, every formal house must have; and the nearer a home resembled a temple the better" (Phillips, *Life and Labor in the Old South* [Boston: Little, Brown, 1929], p. 331).

7. See the discussion of Faulkner's hamlet Frenchman's Bend in chapter 7. The South's larger cities—like Nashville and Richmond—are, of course, geometrical and orthogonal; and a few are even as radial as Washington, D.C. Clement Eaton notes that the greater by far of so-called plantations—fifty percent in Mississippi—were less than two hundred acres (Eaton, *The Growth of Southern Civilization* [New York: Harper and Brothers, 1961], p. 154, n. 10). Eaton here quotes from Herbert Weaver, *Mississippi Farmers, 1850–1860* (Nashville: Vanderbilt University Press, 1945), p. 36.

8. Sidney Fiske Kimball, *Domestic Architecture of the American Colonies and of the Early Republic* (New York: Scribner's, 1922), pp. 78–79.

9. Christian Norberg-Schulz, *Intentions in Architecture* (Cambridge: MIT Press, 1965), p. 146.

10. Giedion describes topological organization as "the free, harmonic disposition of architectonic volumes in space." Giedion, *Architecture and the Phenomenon of Transition*, p. 74.

11. Eaton, *The Growth of Southern Civilization*, p. 122.

12. Miss Hill's comments on the lack of symmetry in the terrace of the Parthenon and in the windows of the Propylea support Doxiades's contention that design was done on site to emphasize the vision of the space from within the site rather than above it. Ida Thallon Hill, *The Ancient City of Athens: Its Topography and Monuments* (London: Methuen, 1953), and K.A. Doxiades, *Architectural Space in Ancient Greece* (Cambridge: MIT Press, 1972). See also Vincent Scully, *The Earth, the Temple, and the Gods: Greek Sacred Architecture*, rev. ed. (New Haven: Yale University Press, 1979), pp. 165–83.

13. Again, see Norberg-Schulz's comment on the Greek notion of the individuality of each architectural element, in *Existence*, p. 61.

14. William Fleming, *Arts and Ideas*, 3rd ed. (New York: Holt, Rinehart and Winston, 1968), pp. 427–28, and Kimball, *Domestic Architecture*, pp. 145–46.

15. Talbot Hamlin, *Greek Revival Architecture in America* (Oxford University Press, 1944; rpt. New York: Dover, 1964), pp. xvi–xvii.

16. What is called "Southern Colonial" is actually Greek Revival style with a free use of Neo-Classical—that is to say Roman—elements. Thomas Jefferson Wertenbaker's succinct historical gloss of the rise of Greek Revival notes its entry into Charleston about 1790–1810. It took firm hold only when Robert Mills took up residence there in 1820 (Wertenbaker, *The Old South: The Founding of American Civilzation* [1942; rpt. New York: Cooper Square, 1963], pp. 283–95). Hamlin, *Greek Revival Architecture in America*, p. 200, notes that it was "not until the later thirties that the example of the superb Mills buildings was commonly followed." Both the factual and the fictive courthouses of Faulkner's county are reflective of this history; the earlier building (ca. 1830), called "simplest Georgian Colonial" (*Requiem for a Nun* [New York: Random House, 1951], p. 40), is remodeled with Neoclassical porticoes after the war.

17. Climate generates "regional character" (Norberg-Schulz, *Intentions*, p. 113), as in the Louisiana "raised" house, but not cultural character. The error in most of this thinking is misattribution. Clement Eaton, for instance (*Growth of Southern Civilization*, p. 119), suggests that one reason for the success of the Greek Revival style was the emphasis on the classics in a gentleman's education. The simple fact is that both study and style were generated from the affinity of cultures.

18. On Jefferson and his contemporaries Lewis Mumford says, "Their love for classic architectural forms went hand in hand with their renewed respect for classic political models" (Mumford, *The South in Architecture* [1941; rpt. New York: Da Capo Press, 1967], p. 49). See also Kimball, *Domestic Architecture*, p. 146.

19. Vitruvius, *The Ten Books on Architecture*, trans. Morris Hicky Morgan (1914; rpt. New York: Dover, 1960), VI, chapter v, section 2 (p. 182).

20. See B. Sprague Allen, *Tides in English Taste, 1619–1800* (New York: Rowman, 1958) I: 24–25.

21. From Davidson, "A Mirror for Artists" in Twelve Southerners, *I'll Take My Stand* (New York: Harper, 1930), p. 55.

22. Francis Pendleton Gaines, *The Southern Plantation: A Study in the Development and the Accuracy of a Tradition* (1924; rpt. Gloucester, Mass.: Peter Smith, 1962), p. 153. Clement Eaton also cites the remarks of Isaac Weld and Benjamin Latrobe on these similarities. See his *Growth*, p. 3.

23. See Allen Guttmann, *The Conservative Tradition in America* (New York: Oxford University Press, 1967), p. 50; Francis Garvin Davenport, *The Myth of Southern History: Historical Consciousness in Twentieth-Century Southern Literature* (Nashville: Vanderbilt University Press, 1970), p. 85; Martin Pawley, "The Time House," in *Meaning in Architecture*, ed. Charles Jencks and George Baird (1965; rpt. New York: George Braziller, 1970), p. 134; and Gaston Bachelard, *The Poetics of Space*, trans. by M. Jolas (1964; rpt. Boston: Beacon Press, 1969), p. 17.

24. Vitruvius, VI, chapter vii, 4: 187.

25. Examples abound. A fine statement of gracious reception is the Concord House in Natchez. J. Frazer Smith notes that the pillars and pediment of the house "formed a shelter for the monumental twin staircase, bordered with wrought iron balustrades meeting at the second floor on a balcony..." (Smith, *White Pillars: Early Life and Architecture of the Lower Mississippi Valley Country* [New York: Bramhall House, 1941], p. 113). See illustrations from Smith, pp. 108, 144. Entrance stairways which receive guests from around a center point are found at many Southern homes, especially in Georgia. See Medora Field Perkerson, *White Columns in Georgia* (New York: Crown, 1952), Wormsloe, p. 11, Holt House, p. 221, the Kirkpatrick home, p. 253, and the Tupper house, p. 266. Clement Eaton remarks that Greek porticoes "were admirably adapted for pleasant conversation and for hospitality" (Eaton, *History of the Old South* [New York: Macmillan, 1966], p. 462). That hospitality was the purpose of such design is obvious, and the classicist even found that Palladio designed villas with such in mind: "Four loggias, which like arms tend to the circumference, seem to receive those who come near the house" (*The Four Books*, II, chap. XVII, p. 55).

26. Much needed is a study of the plantation novel tradition from where Gaines leaves off. Currently there are but two essays on the plantation novel; Gaines's work and Cardwell's piece, "The Plantation House," (see Introduction, n.18), pp. 3–21. There is a thread of the critical tradition through Allen Guttmann's discussion of Washington Irving and others in *The Conservative Tradition in America* (New York: Oxford University Press, 1967) and in "Images of Value and the Sense of the Past" (*New England Quarterly* 35 [1962]: 3–26), Harry Levin's appendix "Castles and Culture" in *The Power of Blackness* (New York: Knopf, 1958), pp. 239–48, and Robert Stallman, *The Houses That James Built and Other Essays* (East Lansing: Michigan State University Press, 1961). These are properly part of the larger critical tradition in fictive architecture.

27. Wertenbaker writes, "There can be no doubt that the South Carolina gentleman put his own tastes, sense of proportion, his personality into his country mansion or his Charleston house not less than the wealthy planters of Virginia or Maryland" [Wertenbaker, *The Old South*, p. 282].

28. Richard M. Weaver, *The Southern Tradition at Bay: A History of Post-Bellum Thought*, ed. George Core and M.E. Bradford (New Rochelle, N.Y.: Arlington House, 1968), p. 57.

Chapter 2

1. It is assumed to correspond geographically with College Hill Station, about the same distance from Oxford on Highway 7.

2. There is a problem about placement of the stairs, and conjecture is precarious here. If the stairway is on the south wall of the hall, it is impossible to see the doorway to the southwest room and nearly impossible to see the kitchen at the northwest corner. If the stairway climbs along the north wall, the southwest doorway is, again, nearly impossible to see. If the northeast room *is* the dining room (as it is unlikely that the kitchen would be diagonal from the dining room), and since Bayard refers to the "back parlor" (p. 80), the "Office" must be the front left or southeast room. The difficulty comes with Louvinia's traversing of the hall. After finishing in the kitchen, she "crossed the hall without looking up and entered the Office..." (p. 19). According to the conjectured plan, she moves from the northwest kitchen to the southeast Office. With the stairs intervening in the hallway, however, she would have to be moving *up* the hallway rather than *across* it. Louvinia could literally cross the hall only if the Office was a back room. If the conjectured plan is accurate and if the text is to be taken literally, Louvinia must then come from the dining room to "cross" the hall to the Office. If

the stairs were on the south wall, with the Office at their foot, Louvinia coming from the kitchen could *cross* the hall, albeit diagonally, to enter the Office, but from Bayard's view at the top of the stairs she would still appear to come up the hall, and be described as such in his narration. Though these details appear trivial, the argument shows that the placement of a room in a plan often turns on the accuracy of a preposition, as in *Sartoris* when Old Bayard tramps *on* [down] the second floor hall to cross it.

3. John's library is of interest and deserves the attention given it by A.S. Bledsoe's "Colonel John Sartoris' Library," *Notes on Mississippi Writers* 7 (1974): 26-29.

4. The boys create in the dirt an imaginative landscape, and although there are no characters, the act of creating the model of Vicksburg is the same process as an author's act of creating fictive landscape in the novel and with the same purpose. Despite the *fact* that Vicksburg has fallen, Bayard can scoop up the pile of woodchips Loosh has scattered, "and set Vicksburg up again" (p. 6). Recreating the real in the model reenacts "the pattern of recapitulant mimic furious victory like a cloth, a shield between us and fact and doom" (p. 4). Faulkner's fictive landscape seeks in the same way to concretize the courage and values of this family in the face of war.

5. *So Red the Rose* (New York: Scribner's, 1934), p. 103. The words are quoted from Donald Davidson's poem "Lee in the Mountains."

6. Francis Garvin Davenport writes: "the mansions stand for a society in which order, permanence, and leisure are still possible. The destruction of many of the large houses by the Northern armies during the Civil War does not negate their symbolic usefulness, but only adds a particular fierceness to memories of their destruction. What they stood for lingers after them in their ruins" (*The Myth of Southern History: Historical Consciousness in Twentieth-Century Southern Literature* [Nashville: Vanderbilt University Press, 1970; North Carolina Press, 1938], p. 85).

7. A *dokimasia* is an examination of magistrates before they take office, as the Aereopagus performed in Ancient Greece; see Pierre Leveque, *The Greek Adventure* (London: Weidenfeld and Nicolson, 1968), p. 176. In this case the would-be magistrates are judged and found wanting.

8. The "fire and fever" at work in *The Unvanquished* is clear from M.E. Bradford's essay "Faulkner's *The Unvanquished*: The High Cost of Survival," *Southern Review* 14 (1978): 428-43.

9. As Ringo draws Sartoris from memory, the Union lieutenant's rational eyes demand a reason for drawing nonexistent houses.

10. Leo Marx's term from his book *The Machine in the Garden: Technology and the Pastoral Ideal in America* (New York: Oxford University Press, 1964), pp. 15-17, 227, 362-63.

Chapter 3

1. There is light coming in the back door of the hall through which Elnora comes when she hears Old Bayard call. She has been working in the kitchen.

2. The same customary arrangement of rooms is assumed for 1919 Sartoris as for its earlier version. In examples of this house form, the music room is usually the right front, the parlor left and the dining room set in the right rear. See J. Frazer Smith, *White Pillars: Early Life and Architecture of the Mississippi Valley Country* (New York: Bramhall House, 1941), Cragfont (p. 29), Marymont (p. 49), Carnton (p. 69), and the reversed example of Arlington (p. 117).

3. This window is the only real contradiction in the plan as conjectured. Neither front room of an east-facing house of this type could have western fenestration, and no other orientation of the house is possible, especially in the light of *Sartoris/Flags in the Dust*. Only the "back parlor" of the earlier house and the dining room of the later one have western windows; neither of them would be called a drawing room. The house reappears later in "There Was a Queen," with the colored glass from Carolina set in one of the library windows. Though the orientation of this house is not given, the stairs are indicated along the left side of the hall by the movements of Elnora and Narcissa.

4. It is as fitting for old Bayard's bedroom to be over this office/library as it is for Miss Jenny's to be above the drawing room, and despite the indication that Bayard's tramping *on* from the top of the stairs to go to his room, other evidence places it above the library.

5. The imaginative reader may look back from *The Unvanquished* to these details and speculate if, for instance, the harness buckle is the one Ringo retrieved from the Union rider he and Bayard shot at, or whether old Bayard's obsession with keys and locks began the night Rosa locked her bedroom door behind them to protect the trunk (*Unvanquished*, p. 47).

6. Dr. Peabody's office in turn stands in contrast to Dr. Alford's, the details of which the narrator notes as "revealing at a glance the proprietor's soul; a soul hampered now by material strictures, but destined and determined some day to function amid Persian rugs and mahogany or teak, and a single irreproachable print on the chaste walls" (p. 94).

7. The "fire of war" element is operative in *Sartoris* as in *The Unvanquished*. The presence of John's ghost in the old pipe recalls the evening Aunt Jenny retold the story of Colonel John's brother Bayard, after which John "leaned forward into the firelight and punched at the blazing logs with the Yankee musket-barrel" (p. 18). Something like a Yankee musket is always stirring up the Sartoris fire, but the image approaches allegory here: the musket-barrel is Yankee-like prodding, the fire is Sartoris fire or fate, and the sparks, which "soared in wild swirling plumes up the chimney" (p. 18) are Bayard's brief flaming career. Sartorises relive their history by stirring up memories —the old fires.

8. Horace and Narcissa's lives are another enclosed space, "a chest of linen" from which "a small sachet of lavender" (Julia Benbow) has been removed (p. 79).

9. Colonel John's flaw might be stated as the attempt to maintain the dream in peacetime with wartime methodology. If he lost the dream in the end, it was not in the seeking of it but in the attempt to maintain it with violence.

10. Gaston Bachelard, *The Poetics of Space*, trans. by M. Jolas (1964; rpt., Boston: Beacon Press, 1969), p. 74.

11. Few pieces of furniture can respond to the relationship they share with their owners as does a piano. For the phenomenology of other such objects see Frederick D. Wilhelmsen's discussion of *agape* and *eros* in his *Metaphysics of Love* (New York: Sheed and Ward, 1962), pp. 80–84.

Chapter 4

1. Christian Norberg-Schulz, *Genius Loci: Towards a Phenomenology of Architecture* (New York: Rizzoli, 1980), p. 77.

2. Though it is tempting to seize on the term "half-acre" in gauging the scale of Sutpen's dwelling, it cannot be considered more than an effective exaggeration. Typical houses of the style average 1500 feet square, the largest of which could not possibly encompass 21,000 square feet.

3. See Frederick D. Wilhelmsen's discussion of the inauthentic lover, in *The Metaphysics of Love* (New York: Sheed and Ward, 1962), pp. 22–36.

4. Merely sitting in a room may be thought of as dwelling in a space, but we actively engage a room when we grasp its doorknob, push open its door, walk across its threshold, and become *in* the room. Chick Mallison's stasis on the threshold of Gavin's study in *Intruder in the Dust* is symbolic of the inception of the investigative task before him. For what seems an eternity to him, he stands "at the door and still holding it, half in the room which he had never actually entered" (*Intruder*, p. 78), trying to engage Gavin in the expedition to dig up Vinson Gowrie's body. At length he gives up, going "out of the room which he had never completely entered anyway . . . releasing the knob for the first time since he had put his hand on it" (*Intruder*, p. 81).

5. Norberg-Schulz, *Genius Loci*, p. 5 and passim.

6. Wilhelmsen, *The Metaphysics of Love*. The following argument is adapted from his discussion of love, pp. 21–23 and 73–84.

7. Later it is Clyte "who spoke but the house itself that said the words" (p. 138), and later still "the house itself speaking again, though it was Judith's voice" (p. 142).

8. The "iron flame" in this passage is of the same species as that of the "iron and fire of civilization" in *Requiem for a Nun* (p. 257), and the fire of war in *The Unvanquished*, which consumes the human and virtuous, leaving nothing but the metal frame, the mechanical, rational parts of things. Here it has indeed met a formidable opponent, and falls back before the fierce, implacable, "impervious and indomitable skeleton" of the mechanical existence which is the structure of Sutpen's existential space.

Chapter 5

1. The assumptions and conclusions brought forth here are drawn from what is known about Jefferson from the Yoknapatawpha canon. Where relevant information is lacking or unclear, I have drawn upon the street design and figure/ground image of Oxford. The image of Oxford is used as a referent—but never as a comparative—only where details of Jefferson necessary to complete the picture are absent. A case in point: Oxford's orientation is predominantly north-south because of its double east-west axis; Jackson and Van Buren avenues cross the square on its north and south edges, respectively, making it only axially symmetrical. Jefferson's orientation is predominantly north-south because most of its fictive traffic enters on this axis, while a side view of the courthouse from the east or west vista never appears in the chronical.

2. The exceptions to topological organization are Miletus, Olynthus, and to a certain extent, Priene.

3. Christian Norberg-Schulz, *Existence, Space and Architecture* (New York: Praeger, 1971), p. 61; Christian Norberg-Schulz, *Intentions in Architecture* (Cambridge: MIT Press, 1965), pp. 143, 151, n.83. On Miletus see R. E. Wycherley, *How the Greeks Built Cities* (London: Macmillan, 1962), pp. 15–29 and A. E. J. Morris, *History of Urban Form: Prehistory to the Renaissance* (New York: Wiley, 1974), pp. 26–29. See also Ferdinando Castagnoli, *Orthogonal Town Planning in Antiquity* (Cambridge: MIT Press, 1971), passim.

4. French, Jere Stuart, *Urban Space: A Brief History of the City Square* (Dubuque: Kendall/Hunt, 1978), p. 56.

5. See Dora Wiebenson's *Sources of Greek Revival Architecture* (London, A. Zwemmer Ltd., 1969), pp. 49–59.

6. Collin Rowe, and John Hejduk, "Lockhart, Texas," *Architectural Record* 121, no. 3 (1957), 203.

7. "Royal Ordinances Concerning the Laying Out of New Towns," as quoted in John Reps, *The Making of Urban America: A History of City Planning in the United States* (Princeton: Princeton University Press, 1965), p. 29. Compare the account of laying out Jefferson and the architect's words, *Requiem*, pp. 38-39. The history of the formation of this code of laws is in Reps's *Cities of the American West: A History of Frontier Urban Planning* (Princeton: Princeton University Press, 1979), pp. 35-40.

8. The authority on the courthouse square is Edward T. Price, Jr. See his "The Central Courthouse Square in the American County Seat," *Geographical Review* 58 (1968), pp. 29-60. The authority on the small town in America and its town square is John Brinckerhoff Jackson, who refers, in discussion and lecture, to Clifton Johnson's *Highways and Byways of Old Dixie* (1905).

9. All these public meeting places have been engendered by this parent of a courthouse, and yet off in the corner of the town is the jail, father of the courthouse, the antithesis of public and communal politics. Later, ironically, it even becomes a *dwelling*, an *oikos*, a structure protecting the basic unit of communal existence, a family.

10. Timgad is the typical example used for discussion of the Roman fortified colonial town. See French, *Urban Space*, p. 55.

11. Evidence for this point is certainly not irrefutable. Sartoris and McCaslin do live north of the town and presumably enter the square via what is North Lamar. Compson's Mile is the southeast quadrant of the town, and Benjy's entry into the square is always up South Lamar. Though Sutpen first entered the town from the south, according to the map in *Absalom* the road from his place joins the west road before it enters the square, as the road from Frenchman's Bend joins the east axis, bringing the Bundrens into Jefferson over the same road Grenier would have traveled. Had Lena Grove entered Oxford's square she would have had to come up South Lamar, since the east entry, Highway 6, joins Lamar south of the square.

Chapter 6

1. Reference is to the Random House edition, 1951.

2. Noel Polk, in his "Alec Holston's Lock and the Founding of Jefferson," *Mississippi Quarterly* 24 (1971): 247-70, contends that the lock is "symbolically the foundation of society" (Polk, p. 253). Though the argument here seems much the same as Polk's, the point is that the lock is a concretization and representative of the principle of law which establishes community.

3. Leveque notes that "[p]articularly amongst the Dorians, the first rulers were leaders of armed bands." The "clandestine departure of pirates outlawed by their city," the "colonization carried out under the authority of a founder," and the honoring of a founder by keeping his name within the town long after its beginnings (Holston), are characteristics which Jefferson's founding shares with early Greek town founding (Pierre Leveque, *The Greek Adventure* [London: Weidenfeld and Nicolson, 1968], p. 185).

4. The biaxial symmetry of Jefferson's town square is an important difference from Oxford's axial symmetry. Though the wanderings of Joe Christmas just off the square in *Light in August* would be possible only in a Harrisonburg type square and not a Lancaster type, the imaginative status of Jefferson permits it to be both. See the discussion of Jefferson and its urban design in the previous chapter.

Chapter 7

1. These three men are linked and contrasted by a fine analogy in *Requiem for a Nun*: "[N]ow there was another newcomer... John Sartoris, with slaves and gear and money too like Grenier and Sutpen, but who was an even better stalemate to Sutpen than Grenier had been because it was apparent at once that he, Sartoris was the sort of man who could even cope with Sutpen in the sense that a man with a sabre or even a small sword and heart enough for it could cope with one with an axe..." (p. 44). Sutpen is the man to beat here. Without someone to "cope with" him, he might have easily overrun the country with his less than ethical designs, and perhaps set less desirable standards for later planters. Though Sartoris is a better stalemate to Sutpen than Grenier, it is not mentioned in what way this is so. Though distance may have been the factor (Grenier's place is more than twenty miles away), the "sabre or even a small sword" analogy suggests that Grenier's gentility may have restrained him from actions Sartoris was less hesitant about, a tendency which is suggested not only by kitchens over kennels at Grenier's, but also by the flamboyant-to-utilitarian range of weapons in the Sartoris attic trunk.

2. *Sanctuary* (Random House, 1951), pp. 6–7. The accounts of Grenier's death conflict here. In *Requiem for a Nun*, he dies two years before the completion of the Jefferson courthouse (p. 44), or about 1836.

3. Except for the McCaslin big house, whose *genius loci* is off-stage and is only the container for the informal gentleman's agreement the McCaslin twins have with their slaves. This mansion is later finished by Buck after he marries Sophonsiba Beauchamp, and will be studied later in the mixed landscape of *Go Down, Moses*.

4. See James B. Meriwether's *The Literary Career of William Faulkner: A Bibliographical Study* (Princeton: Princeton University Press, 1961), pp. 61–62, 70, and Michael Millgate, *The Achievement of William Faulkner* (New York: Random House, 1968), p. 185.

5. The definitive readings of "Barn Burning" are my own master's thesis, "'Like between Two Teams of Horses': Snopes and Sartoris in 'Barn Burning,'" (see Introduction, n.13), and M.E. Bradford's "Family and Community in Faulkner's 'Barn Burning,'" *Southern Review* 17 (1981): 332–39.

6. References to "Barn Burning" are from *Collected Stories* (New York: Random House, 1950), pp. 3–25.

7. The unasked question, of course, is why Will, given his temperament, puts up with the demand or why he even complies. Will very well might simply have said the tobacco was his to begin with and refused to pay. The supposition is that he complies out of his ongoing fear of Snopes's pyromania. That is, if Varner asserts his authority to do what he wants with the goods he takes care of, Flem might do what he pleases with the tenant house, his barn, or even the store itself, with impunity. There is not time, however, even in the long pause before his response, for Will to go through this deduction. So it must be assumed that Will succumbs to simple fear, a hint of defensible extortion.

8. This may be two years after Flem first sits at the gin scales. Ratliff's gallbladder operation and the stories of Flem's cattle herd in Varner's pasture and Eck in the blacksmith shop intervene here and obscure the chronology of events.

9. As Isaac McCaslin dwells lyrically in a natural landscape, Ratliff dwells comically in a communal one. Ratliff, in his seeing and making, is dwelling. From this it may even be said that (since things and places tell both about their own making and the circumstances under

which they were made, and thus also reveal truth) in his seeing and making, Ratliff is himself a place and thus dwells anywhere that he is. (See Christian Norberg-Schulz, *Genius Loci: Towards a Phenomenology of Architecture* [New York: Rizzoli, 1980], p. 185.)

10. The quotation in the heading to this section comes from *The Town*, p. 316. Citations of these last two novels of the Snopes Trilogy are from the Random House editions, pagination preceded by T for *The Town* and M for *The Mansion*. Gavin Stevens's office is "the little quiet dingy mausoleum of human passions" (T, p. 321).

11. We may recall, too, Elnora's praise of Miss Jenny Sartoris, when she says "quality . . . aint is, it's does" ("There Was a Queen," *Collected Stories*, p. 732).

12. The background significance of Cassius's move from rural life to town dwelling has been suggested earlier in this chapter. Though he wants to preserve the values of the wilderness by continuing the annual hunting trips to his camp, he errs (at least in Ike McCaslin's eyes) in thinking he can buy and own a piece of the woods in which to practice those values. After the death of Old Ben, Cassius leases the timber rights to the land. When Ike invites him on a final visit to the Big Bottom, the Major, sitting in his office in Jefferson, declines. Already he has, as Bradford says, one foot in the bank and one in the wilderness (Bradford, in conversation, 1970). With his stock ownership in the bank, very possibly from the revenue of the timber rights, he is no longer a rural man. His rural mansion in "Barn Burning" is still the meaningful and effective symbol of right order, but the old Major's maintenance of it as such is quite conscious and insistent, certainly more so than the less self-conscious effort of John Sartoris in the 1870s. The large but otherwise unpretentious town house in which Manfred lives is the dwelling of a man who is either more subdued in his sense of the symbolic or quite another character from the Cassius de Spain of the "Barn Burning" story.

13. The names Ratliff alludes to here are not people with any ancestral heritage (except perhaps the Astor dynasty) but of other historical parvenus: Yankee patriots and railroad robber barons. Only Hamilton had a house (The Grange) which might have been called aristocratic symbol, but it was hardly ancestral, since his birth was illegitimate.

14. See Gill's discussion of *Castle Rackrent* and other novels of its kind, in *Happy Rural Seat: The English Country House and the Literary Imagination* (New Haven: Yale University Press, 1972), p. 239.

15. This fact is emphasized by Ratliff's recognition that Linda, like Sophonsiba Beauchamp, is just as much a maker of homes as any woman in Faulkner, "naturally interested in the house-building or -remodeling occupation no matter whose it is the same as a bird is interested in the nesting occupation" (T, p. 352). Lena Grove is certainly in this company.

16. The references to Mount Vernon and the style of Robert Adam make this mantel a very insistent allusion to the intricate detail of eighteenth-century interiors, which are so out of style by the late 1920s as to be emblematic of quite gaudy taste. One mantel at Mount Vernon, shipped by Samuel Vaughan from England, was described by Washington himself to be "too elegant and costly by far" (William B. O'Neal, *Architecture in Virginia; An Official Guide to Four Centuries of Building in the Old Dominion* [New York: Walker, 1968], p. 125).

17. For a discussion of the transformation of the Backus-Harriss place and its significance see Mary Mumbach, "'Remaining Must Remain': Patterns of Christian Comedy in Faulkner's *The Mansion*" (Ph.D. dissertation, University of Dallas, 1977).

Chapter 8

1. References are to *Collected Stories* (New York: Random House, 1950).

2. *Intruder in the Dust* (New York: Random House, 1948).

3. Lytle, "The Hind Tit," in *I'll Take My Stand*, pp. 217–18. Thomas Perkins Abernathy's *From Frontier to Plantation in Tennessee: A Study in Frontier Democracy* (Chapel Hill: University of North Carolina Press, 1932) has a complete description of how the basic one-crib cabin was built, and Frank Owsley's *Plain Folk of the Old South* (Baton Rouge: Louisiana State University Press, 1949) quotes an Alabaman's account of building a typical double-log house (pp. 105–7). The best and most accurate commentary on the form and its way of life, however, is Ulrich B. Phillips, *Life and Labor in the Old South* (Boston: Little, Brown, 1929), pp. 328–30. Descriptive details, together with the purpose of each, can be found in John Graves's *Goodbye to a River* (New York: Alfred A. Knopf, 1960), pp. 174–77.

4. J. Frazer Smith, *White Pillars: Early Life and Architecture of the Lower Mississippi Valley Country* (New York: Bramhall House, 1941), pp. 25–26. Mr. Smith's account of the development of Southern frontier housing has stirred up much of the dog-trot house argument. What might be called the evolutionist camp of log-house history argues that the typical great house grew from single-room log cabin to double-crib cabin to hewn-log house, which later was improved with weatherboarding and interior plastering, the passage enclosed and galleries added, or even portico and columns, if the farmer had really, as we say, "arrived." James Patrick maintains, in *Architecture in Tennessee, 1768–1897* (Knoxville: University of Tennessee Press, 1981) and in conversation, that the typical pioneer came to his land from an upcountry cabin and, after setting up a tent or small shack, proceeded immediately, if times were good, to build his great house. The accounts of Lytle and Ulrich Phillips dispute this, but the method here is not as important as the structure, and there were probably sufficient of both instances among those yeomen who were successful enough to become planters to substantiate either side of the argument. The farmer who could establish himself quickly no doubt took Patrick's short route. Thomas Sutpen is Faulkner's example of this case. Those whose rise was slower went from log cabin to separate, sturdier hewn-log house of at least two rooms and galleries, which could later be improved upon. Least likely of all is Frazier Smith's assumption of a single-generation evolution from round log sow's ear cabin to full-blown silk purse pillared mansion.

5. Christian Norberg-Schulz defends the ability of vernacular and even primitive architecture to be symbolic, even in its formal structure. See *Intentions in Architecture* (Cambridge: MIT Press, 1965), p. 185. In the case of the dog-trot house, even Clement Eaton admits that the "homes of the yeoman farmers were symbols of a large measure of economic independence." See his *A History of the Old South,* 2nd ed. (New York: Macmillan, 1966), p. 405.

6. References to *Sartoris* are from the previously cited edition and indicated by an S. References to "The Tall Men" are from *Collected Stories* and are indicated by CS.

7. See Davidson's remarks, noted in chapter 1, on the overly orthodox New England farm where even the barns are painted; in *Still Rebels, Still Yankees* (Baton Rouge: Louisiana State University Press, 1957), pp. 232, 239 and 240.

8. The objects, then, participate in a tropological change (roof for house), a morphological one (hog to hearth), and a teleological one (timekeeper to timepiece). The purpose of the mantel clock involves no functionality, for when old Virginius wants the time he consults "his fat silver watch," not the mantel clock (S, p. 318).

9. In *The Unvanquished*, Bayard Sartoris gives the distance to McCaslin as fifteen miles (p. 52), which would place it closer to town than the MacCallums, even if the MacCallums were, as is said in *Sartoris*, sixteen miles from town (p. 121). No novel speaks of both McCallum and McCaslin, and none of the three published versions of the Yoknapatawpha map shows both places. But Elizabeth Kerr's summary map (in *Yoknapatawpha: Faulkner's 'Little Postage Stamp of Native Soil'* [New York: Fordham University Press, 1976], endpapers), correctly places the MacCallums closer in than McCaslin. The evidence is not only geographical but, as Kerr shows, topological: "In *Sartoris* and 'The Tall Men' the MacCallum farm seems more in the hills than the river bottom, although the 'tall men' grow cotton and raise cattle" (p. 60). McCaslin is a bottom land plantation, as Bayard says in *The Unvanquished* (p. 52).

10. One of Lucas's most obvious errors is his belief that Cass Edmonds had beaten Ike out of his patrimony. In the progress of the suite of stories which is *Go Down, Moses*, the reader first sees Roth through the eyes of Lucas, then the true, more responsible Roth at the conclusion of "The Fire and the Hearth," then later the truth about Ike and his patrimony, and finally Roth's transgression in "Delta Autumn," occurring before the time of "The Fire and the Hearth."

11. See Cleanth Brooks's parallel argument concerning Lucas's wrong opinion of Ike's idealism, in *William Faulkner: The Yoknapatawpha Country* (New Haven: Yale University Press, 1963), p. 254.

12. Christian Norberg-Schulz notes that "the fireplace . . . has since ancient times been the very centre of the dwelling" (*Existence*, p. 32). Faulkner's definitive hearthfire is the Worsham's in the story "Go Down, Moses": "the brick hearth on which the ancient symbol of human coherence and solidarity smoldered" (p. 380).

13. Calvin Brown's *A Glossary of Faulkner's South* (New Haven: Yale University Press, 1976) notes that a back porch is "used primarily as a work-area rather than for relaxation or social purposes" (p. 23). Hence Nat's new back porch is no amenity.

14. The lack of a real door at the back puts the burden of significance on the front one, especially when the McCaslin slaves "voluntarily considered themselves interdict" if they were not out the back door by the time the front one was nailed shut (*Unvanquished*, p. 53). Phenomenologically, no entry is more "open and closed at the same time" or provides for more interaction with the environment than the McCaslin house back entry, permitting the McCaslin slaves to be dwellers of the entire countryside. See Norberg-Schulz on the opening in *Existence*, p. 25.

15. Genuine piety towards the natural world, or what is often called the sacramental view, may be distinguished from more common forms of what J.B. Jackson calls arbolatry, discussed in "The New American Countryside; An Engineered Environment," in *Changing Rural Landscapes*, ed. Erwin H. Zube and Margaret J. Zube (Amherst: University of Massachusetts Press, 1977), p. 27.

16. The literature on the phenomenon of the American wilderness consists of the studies by Leo Marx, Paul Shepard and Roderick Nash. Marx's *The Machine in the Garden* is a well-known and well-done study of the advance of industrial mechanization into the rural agrarian or even uninhabited landscape. Paul Shepard's *Man in the Landscape: A Historic View of the Esthetics of Nature* (New York: Alfred A. Knopf, 1967) is a suite of essays on man's views of the natural world, especially since the Middle Ages, with some consideration of phenomena such as mountain and cave. Roderick Nash's *Wilderness and the American Mind* (rev. ed., New Haven: Yale University Press, 1973) is a thorough and scholarly study

of nearly everything thought and written about wilderness since ancient times. Nash finds the development of two approaches to the American wilderness: the Puritan frontier view of a cursed wasteland to be conquered and tamed, and the eighteenth-century picture of sublime beauty and grandeur, evidence of divine creation though not necessarily divine presence. The Biblical referent to Faulkner's wilderness—if it requires one—is the wilderness of Revelation, which "enables the contemplative Christian to see the Divine more clearly, unemcumbered by the world" (Tuan, *Topophilia* [Englewood Cliffs, N.J.: Prentice-Hall, 1974], p. 110).

17. On the Yoknapatawpha wilderness there is John Pilkington's "Nature's Legacy to William Faulkner," in *The South and Faulkner's Yoknapatawpha: the Actual and the Apocryphal,* ed. Evans Harrington and Ann J. Abadie (Jackson: University Press of Mississippi, 1977), pp. 104–27, is representative of this view.

18. More about these spirits and their classical origins can be gleaned from such pieces as John R. Stilgoe's "Hobgoblin in Suburbia" (*Landscape Architecture* 73, no.6 (1983): 54–61) than from even so excellent studies as those of Nash, Marx, Shepard, or Tuan.

19. Citations in this section are from the first edition of *Go Down, Moses* (New York: Random House, 1941).

20. The drawings of Edward Shenton in *Big Woods* (New York: Random House, 1955) are fine representations of the scale of the woods.

21. Robert Venturi's term, in *Complexity and Contradiction in Architecture* (New York: Museum of Modern Art, 1977), p. 86.

22. Bollnow suggests that the forest is "generally experienced as being simultaneously closed and open" (In Norberg-Schulz, *Existence*, p. 34).

23. A note on the phenomenology of the condition of *being* in a place: the meaning of a place as perceived from the condition of being in it has a permanence like that of myth, regardless of previous factual or historical existence. The meaning of a place can be retained as an image in the memory, and that image, recalled in a similar place, can invest it with the meaning of the place remembered, thus recovering the place itself by reestablishing the condition of being in it to the person who recalls it from his memory.

24. Norberg-Schulz, *Existence*, p. 32.

25. A domain, again, is a more familiar area, qualitatively known and structured by means of paths and places. See Norberg-Schulz, *Existence*, pp. 23–24.

26. Norberg-Schulz's comments on rivers are specifically applicable here: "A river may be said to separate and unify simultaneously. It divides the land, but also defines a space which is common to both shores. The unifying effect is usually strengthened by the land sloping down towards the water, and by the river serving as a means of communication.... Here [man] feels outside and inside, free and protected at the same time, moving back and forth between two domains which are different, although belonging to the same totality (*Existence*, pp. 53–54).

27. See chapter 4 of this study for the geographical location of Sutpen's Hundred and his fishing camp.

28. Paul Shepard writes: "One of the fancied dangers of being the first into a wilderness was getting lost. The idea of the absence of landmarks and loss of orientation approaches the theme of the vision and the infinite and almost always evokes an awareness of silence" (*Man in the Landscape*, p. 181).

29. Norberg-Schulz, *Genius Loci*, p. 22.

30. As McCaslin has one foot in a farm and the other in a bank, De Spain has, as said before, one foot in the bank and the other in the wilderness.

Chapter 9

1. See Introduction, p. 9, n.18.

2. Watson, "Faulkner: The House of Fiction," p. 150, in Doreen Fowler and Ann J. Abadie, eds., *Fifty Years of Yoknapatawpha: Faulkner and Yoknapatawpha, 1979* (Jackson: University Press of Mississippi, 1980).

3. This image is a relative of Dostoevsky's rendering of the Russian troika. Image is just one of several tropes through which fictive space expresses meaning.

4. I mean this in the sense that someone in a room with his hand on a freestanding wall may inhabit the room, until he touches a support pillar and perceives himself, though in the same spot, to be inhabiting the entire building.

5. There is much more involved in this analogy than there is space to discuss here. Others may choose to note the parallels between constellations rotating through zodiacal pastures and the seasonal rotation of grazing stock through zoological or agrarian pastures.

6. See Christian Norberg-Schulz's taxonomy of spaces in *Existence, Space and Architecture* (New York: Praeger, 1971), p. 11.

Appendix

1. It is important here to avoid notions of a Southern "mind" of the kind refuted by Donald Davidson in his "Mr. Cash and the Proto-Dorian South," in *Still Rebels, Still Yankees*, pp. 191–212.

2. Richard M. Weaver, "The South and the American Union," in *The Lasting South: Fourteen Southerners Look at Their Home*, ed. Louis D. Rubin, Jr. and James Jackson Kilpatrick (Chicago: Henry Regnery, 1957), p. 50. Weaver refers to Vernon L. Parrington's *The Romantic Revolution in America*, vol. II of *Main Currents in American Thought* (New York: Harcourt, Brace, and World, 1954), especially pp. 70–81.

3. Francis Pendleton Gaines, *The Southern Plantation: A Study in the Development and the Accuracy of a Tradition* (1924; rpt. Gloucester, Mass.: Peter Smith, 1962), p. 155.

4. A special issue of *Southern Humanities Review* 11 (1977), entitled "The Classical Tradition in the South," seems to be the first concentrated effort.

5. A suggestion of the plentitude of such evidence is given by Richard M. Gummere's book, *The American Colonial Mind and the Classical Tradition: Essays in Comparative Culture* (Cambridge: Harvard University Press, 1963). A particular example is John Randolph's famous letter to Dudley on Trajan and Antoninus as exemplars of responsibility for the rich, wise, and powerful man, quoted in Russell Kirk's *John Randolph of Roanoak*, rev. ed. (Chicago: Henry Regnery, 1964), p. 168.

6. Owsley, in Twelve Southerners, *I'll Take My Stand* (New York: Harper and Brothers, 1980), pp. 70–71.

7. As an agrarian society, he maintains earlier, the South had the same way of life for which Egypt, Greece, Rome, England, and France had stood; i.e., the *ideal* of agrarian life (Owsley, in *I'll Take My Stand*, p. 69).

8. Gummere, *The American Colonial Mind*, p. 37.

9. Frank Owsley, *Plain Folk of the Old South* (Baton Rouge: Louisiana State University Press, 1949), p. 95. The personal ramifications of the sense of family are eloquently stated by Stark Young in "Not in Memoriam, but in Defense," in *I'll Take My Stand*, pp. 346–47, and by his character Hugh McGehee, in *So Red the Rose*, p. 395.

10. See Charles Norris Cochrane, *Christianity and Classical Culture: A Study of Thought and Action from Augustus to Augustine* (New York: Oxford University Press, 1957), pp. 60–61. Greeks as a people celebrated a festival of men who had the same father; a kind of national recognition of the family as the ground of society. See Pierre Leveque, *The Greek Adventure* (London: Weidenfeld and Nicolson, 1968), p. 174.

11. See Leveque, *Greek Adventure*, p. 464 and Cochrane, *Christianity*, p. 50.

12. See Cochrane, *Christianity*, pp. 60–61 and p. 46, respectively.

13. M.E. Bradford, "Faulkner's Doctrine of Nature: A Study of the 'Endurance' Theme in the Yoknapatawpha Fiction" (Ph.D. diss., Vanderbilt, 1968), pp. 80f.

14. Leveque, *Greek Adventure*, p. 107. Voegelin's description is more specific but still comparable: the king was a noble whose position depended on his recognized superiority through noble ancestry, wealth, strength, and intelligence. Political organs of such a region were a king, a council, and a popular assembly (*agore*) of arms-bearing freemen. (*World of the Polis*, vol. 2 of Order and History [Baton Rouge: Louisiana State University Press, 1957], p. 77.)

15. Leveque, *Greek Adventure*, p. 47.

16. Leveque, *Greek Adventure*, p. 102.

17. Gaines, *The Southern Plantation*, p. 153.

18. Cochrane on Aristotle in *Christianity*, p. 49.

19. Richard Weaver cites General John Mason's testimony on the plantation as "a relatively self-sufficient community" (*The Southern Tradition at Bay: A History of Post-Bellum Thought*, ed. George Coe and M.E. Bradford [New Rochelle, N.Y.: Arlington House, 1968], p. 51).

20. See Bradford, "Faulkner's Doctrine of Nature," p. 84, n.14.

21. Leveque, *Greek Adventure*, p. 41.

22. Johnson, as quoted in Weaver's, *The Southern Tradition at Bay*, p. 354.

23. Leveque, *Greek Adventure*, p. 130f. His description of the Ionian amphictyony sounds remarkably like one of the South: "a better climate than any other we know of," according to Herodotus (I, 142), a fertile soil, an incentive to commercial life in its position on a coast where oriental products abounded, the same dialect spoken everywhere—with some slight differences which Herodotus mentions—and institutions which were generally closely related by a common origin... (p. 138).

24. Cochrane, *Christianity*, pp. 60–61.

25. Leveque, *Greek Adventure*, pp. 237, 353.

26. Eric Voegelin notes that after the reform of Cleisthenes "only the power of the aristocratic *gene* was broken, not the gentilitian spirit of the institutions. The *demos*, in spite of its

territorial basis, was a corporation of persons just like the older blood-relationships" (*World of the Polis*, vol. 2 of Order and History [Baton Rouge: Louisiana State University Press, 1957], p. 116).

27. C.M. Bowra, *The Greek Experience* (New York: World Publishing Co., 1957), p. 73.

28. Cochrane, *Christianity*, p. 46.

29. Cochrane, *Christianity*, pp. 46–47.

30. William R. Taylor, *Cavalier and Yankee: The Old South and the American National Character* (New York: George Braziller, 1961), p. 82.

31. Vernon L. Parrington, *1800–1860: The Romantic Revolution in America*, vol. 2, Main Currents in American Thought (1927; rpt. New York: Harcourt, Brace and World, 1954), p. 64.

32. Parrington, *Currents*, p. 78.

33. Taylor, *Cavalier and Yankee*, p. 58.

34. Taylor, *Cavalier and Yankee*, pp. 82–83.

35. Ransom, "Reconstructed but Unregenerate," in *I'll Take My Stand*, p. 14. Francis B. Simkins also notes that the absence of strict class lines was similar to Greek democratic society (*The Everlasting South* [Baton Rouge: Louisiana State University Press, 1963], p. 39).

36. See Leveque, *Greek Adventure*, p. 179. The yeoman farmer has much in common with the Spartan *perioikoi*—a freeman who farmed the less fertile hill country and "cultivated the land, raised sheep and pigs, and practiced trade and handicrafts. They were grouped in rough market towns . . . and enjoyed a large degree of autonomy but no rights with regard to city policy" (p. 163).

37. Cochrane, *Christianity*, pp. 35–37, 62.

38. The phrase is both Weaver's (*Southern Tradition at Bay*, p. 104) and Tate's (*Essays*, pp. 571–73).

39. Weaver, in Louis D. Rubin and James Jackson Kilpatrick, eds., *The Lasting South: Fourteen Southerners Look at Their Home* (Chicago: Henry Regnery, 1957), p. 64.

40. See Allen Tate, *Essays of Four Decades* (Chicago: Swallow Press, 1968), pp. 571–73.

41. Weaver, *The Southern Tradition at Bay*, p. 103.

42. Weaver, *The Southern Tradition at Bay*, pp. 111, 105. See also Randall Stewart, *American Literature and Christian Doctrine* (Louisiana State University Press, 1958), p. 14.

43. The nature of Southern piety has been excellently articulated by many of its practitioners. Since the subject is the classical virtue of piety, which is the same in both cultures, its nature will not be detailed here. See Weaver on the general nature of Southern piety, how it accommodates contingency and conduces humility through acceptance of the inscrutability of nature (*The Southern Tradition at Bay*, pp. 32–34 and his "Aspects of the Southern Philosophy," in *Southern Renascence: The Literature of the Modern South*, ed. Louis D. Rubin, Jr., and Robert D. Jacobs [Baltimore: The Johns Hopkins Press, 1953], pp. 15, 20), John Crowe Ransom on piety towards nature and the Natural Law (*I'll Take My Stand*, p. 7), and Louise Cowan's "The 'Pietas' of Southern Poetry," in *South: Modern Southern Literature in Its Cultural Setting*, edited by Louis D. Rubin, Jr. and Robert D. Jacobs (Garden City, NY: Doubleday, 1961), pp. 95–114.

44. Leveque, *Greek Adventure,* p. 231.

45. The term is Frederick Wilhelmsen's. See the chapter "Cicero and the Politics of the Public Orthodoxy," in his *Christianity and Political Philosophy* (Athens, Georgia: University of Georgia Press, 1978), pp. 25–59, from which can be sythesized the following definition: the public orthodoxy is the matrix of judgments and convictions, enshrined in custom and folkways, embodied in literary form (formally in charter and constitution or informally in an epic literature), defining the good life and the meaning of human existence as conceived by that particular society, which sees in it the character of their way of life and the destiny of their society.

46. Weaver, *The Southern Tradition at Bay,* p. 98.

47. Leveque, *Greek Adventure,* p. 289.

48. De Forest, in J.B. Hubbell, *The South in American Literature, 1607–1900* (Durham: Duke University Press, 1954), p. 395.

49. Gildersleeve, quoted in Weaver, *The Southern Tradition at Bay,* p. 361.

50. See C.M. Bowra, *Periclean Athens* (New York: Dial Press, 1971), pp. 37–38.

51. Davidson, "Mr. Cash and the Proto-Dorian South," in *Still Rebels, Still Yankees* (Baton Rouge: Louisiana State University Press, 1957), p. 195.

52. See Leveque, *Greek Adventure,* pp. 121–22, 177.

53. See Cochrane, *Christianity,* p. 62.

54. Leveque's description of the effects of the conquest of Troy is in many ways applicable to the American South. See Leveque, *Greek Adventure,* p. 52.

55. The Athenian political policy of "intransigent imperialism" (Leveque, *Greek Adventure,* p. 269) during this period supports Gildersleeve's alignment of Athens with the North. Also, Sparta was the more traditional, customary, and military society. The defeat of Athens, however, realigns it with the South.

56. Leveque, *Greek Adventure,* p. 329.

57. See Louis B. Wright, *The First Gentlemen of Virginia: Intellectual Qualities of the Early Colonial Ruling Class* (1940; rpt., Charlottesville: University Press of Virginia, 1964), pp. 66–67 and p. 66, n.5.

58. Wright, *First Gentlemen,* pp. 128, 212. Leveque, *Greek Adventure,* p. 108.

59. Hubbell, *The South in American Literature,* p. 47 and Gummere, *The American Colonial Mind,* pp. 85, 86.

60. Leveque, *Greek Adventure,* p. 289. The predominance of political literature over *belle lettres* in the early South was a natural consequence of the concern for maintaining the moral norm, and these too have referents in Demosthenean Greece. See Leveque, *Greek Adventure,* pp. 355 and 379.

61. Leveque, *Greek Adventure,* p. 467.

62. Bowra, *The Greek Experience,* p. 73.

63. Leveque, *Greek Adventure,* p. 174.

64. Leveque, *Greek Adventure,* p. 108.

Bibliography

Works by Faulkner

Absalom, Absalom! New York: Modern Library, 1951.
Big Woods. New York: Random House, 1955.
Collected Stories. New York: Random House, 1950.
Flags in the Dust. New York: Random House, 1973.
Go Down, Moses. New York: Random House, 1942.
The Hamlet. New York: Random House, 1958.
Intruder in the Dust. New York: Random House, 1948.
The Mansion. New York: Random House, 1959.
Requiem for a Nun. New York: Random House, 1951.
Sartoris. New York: Random House, 1929.
The Town. New York: Random House, 1957.
The Unvanquished. New York: Random House, 1966.

Related Criticism

Abernathy, Thomas Perkins. *From Frontier to Plantation in Tennessee: A Study in Frontier Democracy.* Chapel Hill: University of North Carolina Press, 1932.
――――. *The South in the New Nation: 1789–1819.* Baton Rouge: Louisiana State University Press, 1961.
Aiken, Charles. "Faulkner's Yoknapatawpha County: A Place in the American South." *Geographical Review* 69 (1979): 331–48.
――――. "Faulkner's Yoknapatawpha County: Geographical Fact into Fiction." *Geographical Review* 67 (1977): 1–21.
Alden, John Richard. *The First South.* Baton Rouge: Louisiana State University Press, 1961.
Allen, B. Sprague. *Tides in English Taste: 1619–1800.* Vol. 1. New York: Rowman, 1958.
Allister, Mark. "Faulkner's Aristocratic Families: The Grand Design and the Plantation House." *Midwest Quarterly* 25 (1983): 90–101.
Bachelard, Gaston. *The Poetics of Space.* Translated by M. Jolas. 1964. Reprint. Boston: Beacon Press, 1969.
Bledsoe, A.S. "Colonel John Sartoris' Library." *Notes on Mississippi Writers* 7 (1974): 26–29.
Bloomer, Kent and Moore, Charles W. *Body, Memory, and Architecture.* New Haven: Yale University Press, 1977.
Blotner, Joseph. *Faulkner: A Biography.* 2 vols. New York: Random House, 1974.
Bollnow, Otto F. "Lived Space." In *Readings in Existential Phenomenology,* edited by Nathaniel Lawrence and Daniel O'Connor, 178–86. Englewood Cliffs, N.J.: Prentice-Hall, 1967.

Bowra, C.M. *The Greek Experience*. New York: World Publishing Co., 1957.

_____. *Periclean Athens*. New York: Dial Press, 1971.

Bradford, M.E. "Family and Community in Faulkner's 'Barn Burning.'" *Southern Review* 17 (1981): 332–39.

_____. "Faulkner's Doctrine of Nature: A Study of the 'Endurance' Theme in the Yoknapatawpha Novels." Ph.D. diss., Vanderbilt University, 1968.

_____. "Faulkner's *The Unvanquished*: The High Cost of Survival." *Southern Review* 14 (1978): 428–43.

_____. "The Gum Tree Scene: Observations on the Structure of 'The Bear.'" *Southern Humanities Review* 1 (1967): 147–50.

Brooks, Cleanth. *William Faulkner: The Yoknapatawpha Country*. New Haven: Yale University Press, 1963.

Brown, Calvin S. *A Glossary of Faulkner's South*. New Haven: Yale University Press, 1976.

Cardwell, Guy A. "The Plantation House: An Analogical Image." *Southern Literary Journal* 2 (1969): 3–21.

Castagnoli, Ferdinando. *Orthogonal Town Planning in Antiquity*. Cambridge: MIT Press, 1971.

Coates, Robert M. *The Outlaw Years: The History of the Land Pirates of the Natchez Trace*. New York: Literary Guild of America, 1930.

Cochrane, Charles Norris. *Christianity and Classical Culture: A Study of Thought and Action from Augustus to Augustine*. New York: Oxford University Press, 1957.

Couch, W .T., ed. *Culture in the South*. Chapel Hill: University of North Carolina Press, 1934.

Coulter, E. Merton and Stephenson, Wendell Holmes, eds. *A History of the South*. Vol. 7: *The Confederate States of America, 1861–1865*, and Vol. 8: *The South during Reconstruction, 1865–1877*. Baton Rouge: Louisiana State University Press, 1950.

Crane, John K. "The Jefferson Courthouse: An *Axis Exsecrabilis Mundi*." *Twentieth Century Literature* 15 (1969): 19–23.

Craven, Avery O. *The Growth of Southern Nationalism, 1848–1861*. A History of the South, vol. 6. Edited by E. Merton Coulter and and Wendell Holmes Stephenson. Baton Rouge: Louisiana State University Press, 1953.

Davenport, Francis Garvin. *The Myth of Southern History: Historical Consciousness in Twentieth-Century Southern Literature*. Nashville: Vanderbilt University Press, 1970. North Carolina Press, 1938.

Davidson, Donald. *Still Rebels, Still Yankees*. Baton Rouge: Louisiana State University Press, 1957.

Doxiadis, Konstantinos A. *Architectural Space in Ancient Greece*. Cambridge: MIT Press, 1972.

Eaton, Clement. *The Growth of Southern Civilization*. New York: Harper and Brothers, 1961.

_____. *A History of the Old South*. 2nd ed. New York: Macmillan, 1966.

Fisher, Richard E. "The Wilderness, the Commissary, and the Bedroom: Faulkner's Ike McCaslin as Hero in a Vacuum." *English Studies* 44 (1963): 19–28.

Fleming, William. *Arts and Ideas*. 3rd ed. New York: Holt, Rinehart and Winston, 1968.

Fowler, Doreen and Abadie, Ann J., eds. *Fifty Years of Yoknapatawpha: Faulkner and Yoknapatawpha, 1979*. Jackson: University Press of Mississippi, 1980.

French, Jere Stuart. *Urban Space: A Brief History of the City Square*. Dubuque, Iowa: Kendall/Hunt, 1978.

Gaines, Francis Pendleton. *The Southern Plantation: A Study in the Development and the Accuracy of a Tradition*. 1924. Reprint. Gloucester, Mass.: Peter Smith, 1962.

Gates, Allen. "The Old Frenchman Place: Symbol of a Lost Civilization." *Iowa English Yearbook* 13 (1968): 44–50.

Giedion, Sigfried. *Architecture and the Phenomenon of Transition: The Three Space Concepts in Architecture*. Cambridge: Harvard University Press, 1971.

_____. *The Beginnings of Architecture.* The Eternal Present, vol. 6. New York: Random House, 1964.

_____. *Space, Time and Architecture: The Growth of a New Tradition.* Cambridge: Harvard University Press, 1943.

Gill, Richard. *Happy Rural Seat: The English Country House and the Literary Imagination.* New Haven: Yale University Press, 1972.

Girouard, Mark. *Life in the English Country House: A Social and Cultural History.* New Haven: Yale University Press, 1978.

_____. *The Victorian Country House.* Revised edition. New Haven: Yale University Press, 1979.

Graves, John. *Goodbye to a River.* New York: Alfred A. Knopf, 1960.

Gropius, Walter. *Apollo in the Democracy: The Cultural Obligation of the Architect.* New York: McGraw-Hill, 1968.

Gummere, Richard M. *The American Colonial Mind and the Classical Tradition: Essays in Comparative Culture.* Cambridge: Harvard University Press, 1963.

Guttmann, Allen. *The Conservative Tradition in America.* New York: Oxford University Press, 1967.

_____. "Images of Value and the Sense of the Past." *New England Quarterly* 35 (1962): 3–26.

Hamlin, Talbot Faulkner. *Greek Revival Architecture in America.* 1944. Reprint. New York: Dover, 1964.

Heidegger, Martin. *Poetry, Language, Thought.* New York: Harper and Row, 1975.

Henneman, John Bell, ed. *History of the Literary and Intellectual Life of the South.* The South in the Building of the Nation, vol. 7. Edited by Samuel Chiles Mitchell. Richmond: The Southern Historical Publication Society, 1909.

Hill, Ida Thallon. *The Ancient City of Athens: Its Topography and Monuments.* London: Methuen, 1953.

Howell, Elmo. "Faulkner's Country Church: A Note on 'Shingles for the Lord.'" *Mississippi Quarterly* 21 (1968): 205–10.

Hubbell, Jay B. *The South in American Literature, 1607–1900.* Durham: Duke University Press, 1954.

Jackson, John Brinckerhoff. *The Necessity for Ruins, and Other Topics.* Amherst: University of Massachusetts Press, 1980.

Jager, Bernd. "The Space of Dwelling: A Phenomenological Exploration." *Humanitas* 12 (1976): 311–31.

Jencks, Charles and Baird, George, eds. *Meaning in Architecture.* 1965. Reprint. New York: George Braziller, 1970.

Kerr, Elizabeth. *Yoknapatawpha: Faulkner's 'Little Postage Stamp of Native Soil.'* New York: Fordham University Press, 1976.

Kimball, Sidney Fiske. *Domestic Architecture of the American Colonies and of the Early Republic.* New York: Scribner's, 1922.

Kirk, Russell. *John Randolph of Roanoke.* Revised edition. Chicago: Henry Regney, 1964.

Leveque, Pierre. *The Greek Adventure.* London: Weidenfeld and Nicolson, 1968.

Levin, Harry. *The Power of Blackness.* New York: Knopf, 1958.

Lytle, Andrew. *The Hero with the Private Parts.* Baton Rouge: Louisiana State University Press, 1966.

Marx, Leo. *The Machine in the Garden: Technology and the Pastoral Ideal in America.* New York: Oxford University Press, 1964.

McClung, William A. *The Country House in English Renaissance Poetry.* Berkeley: University of California Press, 1977.

Meriwether, James B. *The Literary Career of William Faulkner: A Bibliographical Study.* Princeton: Princeton University Press, 1961.

Metcalf, J.C. "Architecture in the South." In *History of the Social Life of the South*. The South in the Building of the Nation, vol. 10, Edited by Samuel Chiles Mitchell. Richmond: The Southern Historical Publication Society, 1909.

Millgate, Michael. *The Achievement of William Faulkner*. New York: Random House, 1968.

Morris, A.E.J. *History of Urban Form: Prehistory to the Renaissance*. New York: Wiley, 1974.

Mumbach, Mary. "'Remaining Must Remain': Patterns of Christian Comedy in Faulkner's *The Mansion*." Ph.D. diss., University of Dallas, 1977.

Mumford, Lewis. *The South in Architecture*. 1941. Reprint. New York: Da Capo Press, 1967.

Nash, Roderick. *Wilderness and the American Mind*. Revised edition. New Haven: Yale University Press, 1973.

Norberg-Schulz, Christian. *Existence, Space and Architecture*. New York: Praeger, 1971.

_____. *Genius Loci: Towards a Phenomenology of Architecture*. New York: Rizzoli, 1980.

_____. *Intentions in Architecture*. Cambridge: MIT Press, 1965.

_____. *Meaning in Western Architecture*. New York: Praeger, 1974.

O'Neal, William B. *Architecture in Virginia: An Official Guide to Four Centuries of Building in the Old Dominion*. New York: Walker, 1968.

Owsley, Frank. *Plain Folk of the Old South*. Baton Rouge: Louisiana State University Press, 1949.

Palladio, Andrea. *The Four Books of Architecture*. 1932. Reprint. New York: Dover, 1960.

Parrington, Vernon L. *1800–1860: The Romantic Revolution in America*. Main Currents in American Thought, vol. 2. 1927. Reprint. New York: Harcourt, Brace and World, 1954.

Patrick, James. *Architecture in Tennessee: 1768–1897*. Knoxville: University of Tennessee Press, 1981.

Perkerson, Medora Field. *White Columns in Georgia*. New York: Crown Publishers, 1952.

Phillips, Ulrich B. *Life and Labor in the Old South*. Boston: Little, Brown, 1929.

Polk, Noel. "Alec Holston's Lock and the Founding of Jefferson." *Mississippi Quarterly* 24 (1971): 247–70.

_____. "The Critics and Faulkner's 'Little Postage Stamp of Native Soil.'" *Mississippi Quarterly* 23 (1970): 323–35.

Price, Edward T., Jr. "The Central Courthouse Square in the American County Seat." *Geographical Review* 58 (1968): 29–60.

Reps, John William. *Cities of the American West: A History of Frontier Urban Planning*. Princeton: Princeton University Press, 1979.

_____. *The Making of Urban America: A History of City Planning in the United States*. Princeton: Princeton University Press, 1965.

_____. *Town Planning in Frontier America*. Princeton: Princeton University Press, 1970.

Rowe, Collin and Hejduk, John. "Lockhart, Texas." *Architectural Record* 121, no. 3 (1957): 201–6.

Rubin, Louis D., Jr. and Jacobs, Robert D., eds. *South: Modern Southern Literature in Its Cultural Setting*. Garden City, N.Y.: Johns Hopkins University Press, 1953.

_____. *Southern Renascence: The Literature of the Modern South*. Baltimore: Johns Hopkins Press, 1953.

Rubin, Louis D., Jr., and Kilpatrick, James Jackson, eds. *The Lasting South: Fourteen Southerners Look at Their Home*. Chicago: Henry Regnery, 1957.

Ruzicka, William T. "'Like between Two Teams of Horses': Snopes and Sartoris in 'Barn Burning.'" Master's thesis, University of Dallas, 1970.

Schwarz, Rudolf. *The Church Incarnate: The Sacred Function of Christian Architecture*. Chicago: Henry Regnery, 1958.

Scully, Vincent. *The Earth, the Temple, and the Gods: Greek Sacred Architecture*. Revised edition. New Haven: Yale University Press, 1979.

Shepard, Paul. *Man in the Landscape: A Historic View of the Esthetics of Nature.* New York: Alfred A. Knopf, 1967.

Simkins, Francis B. *The Everlasting South.* Baton Rouge: Louisiana State University Press, 1963.

Slabey, Robert M. "Faulkner's Geography and Hightower's House." *American Notes and Queries* 3 (1965): 85–86.

Smith, J. Frazer. *White Pillars: Early Life and Architecture of the Lower Mississippi Valley Country.* New York: Bramhall House, 1941.

Stallman, Robert. *The Houses That James Built and Other Essays.* Athens: Ohio University Press, 1977.

Stewart, Randall. *American Literature and Christian Doctrine.* Baton Rouge: Louisiana State University Press, 1958.

———. *Regionalism and Beyond: Essays of Randall Stewart.* Edited by George Core. Nashville: Vanderbilt University Press, 1968.

Sydnor, Charles S. *The Development of Southern Sectionalism, 1819–1848.* A History of the South, vol. 5. Edited by E. Merton Coulter and Wendell Holmes Stephenson. Baton Rouge: Louisiana State University Press, 1948.

Tate, Allen. *Essays of Four Decades.* Chicago: Swallow Press, 1968.

Taylor, William R. *Cavalier and Yankee: The Old South and the American National Character.* New York: George Braziller, 1961.

Tuan, Yi-Fu. *Space and Place: The Perspective of Experience.* Minneapolis: University of Minnesota Press, 1977.

———. *Topophilia: A Study of Environmental Perception, Attitudes, and Values.* Englewood Cliffs, N.J.: Prentice-Hall, 1974.

Twelve Southerners. *I'll Take My Stand.* New York: Harper and Brothers, 1930.

Venturi, Robert. *Complexity and Contradiction in Architecture.* New York: Museum of Modern Art, 1977.

Vitruvius Pollio, Marcus. *The Ten Books on Architecture.* Translated by Morris Hicky Morgan. 1914. Reprint. New York: Dover, 1960.

Voegelin, Eric. *The World of the Polis.* Order and History, vol. 2. Baton Rouge: Louisiana State University Press, 1957.

Weaver, Herbert. *Mississippi Farmers, 1850–1860.* Nashville: Vanderbilt University Press, 1945.

Weaver, Richard M. *The Southern Tradition at Bay: A History of Post-Bellum Thought.* Edited by George Core and M.E. Bradford. New Rochelle, N.Y.: Arlington House, 1968.

Welty, Eudora. *Place in Fiction.* New York: House of Books, 1957.

Wertenbaker, Thomas Jefferson. *The Old South: The Founding of American Civilization.* 1942. Reprint. New York: Cooper Square, 1963.

———. *The Shaping of Colonial Virginia.* 3 works in 1 vol. New York: Russell and Russell, 1958.

Wiebenson, Dora. *Sources of Greek Revival Architecture.* London: A. Zwemmer, 1969.

Wilhelmsen, Frederick D. *Christianity and Political Philosophy.* Athens, Georgia: University of Georgia Press, 1978.

———. *The Metaphysics of Love.* New York: Sheed and Ward, 1962.

Wright, Lewis B. *The First Gentlemen of Virginia: Intellectual Qualities of the Early Colonial Ruling Class.* 1940. Reprint. Charlottesville: University Press of Virginia, 1964.

Wycherley, R. E. *How the Greeks Built Cities.* London: Macmillan, 1962.

Young, Thomas Daniel, Watkins, Floyd C., and Beatty, Richmond Croom, eds. *The Literature of the South.* Revised edition. Glenview, Ill.: Scott, Foresman, 1968.

Zube, Ervin H., ed. *Landscapes: Selected Writings of J. B. Jackson.* Amherst: University of Massachusetts Press, 1970.

———, and Zube, Margaret J., eds. *Changing Rural Landscapes.* Amherst: University of Massachusetts Press, 1977.

Index